THE BAFFLED PARENT'S GUIDE TO

COACHING GIRLS'
SOCCER

Look for these other Baffled Parent's Guides

Coaching Youth Baseball
by Bill Thurston

Great Baseball Drills
by Jim Garland

Coaching Youth Basketball
by David G. Faucher

Great Basketball Drills
by Jim Garland

Coaching Youth Football
by Paul Pasqualoni with Jim McLaughlin

Coaching Youth Hockey
by Bruce Driver with Clare Wharton

Teaching Kids Golf
by Detty Moore

Coaching Boys' Lacrosse
by Greg Murrell and Jim Garland

Coaching Girls' Lacrosse
by Janine Tucker and Maryalice Yakutchik

Coaching Six-and-Under Soccer
by David Williams and Scott Graham

Coaching Youth Soccer
by Bobby Clark

Great Soccer Drills
by Tom Fleck and Ron Quinn

Coaching Youth Softball
by Jacquie Joseph

Coaching Tee Ball
by Bing Broido

THE BAFFLED PARENT'S
GUIDE TO
COACHING GIRLS'
SOCCER

Drayson Hounsome

Head Women's Soccer Coach
Long Island University/CW Post Campus

Photos by
Bruce Curtis

Mc Graw Hill

Camden, Maine • New York • Chicago • San Francisco
Lisbon • London • Madrid • Mexico City • Milan
New Delhi • San Juan • Seoul • Singapore • Sydney • Toronto

To my Mum and Dad, the two most loving people in the world, who have supported and encouraged me in everything I have done.

The McGraw·Hill Companies

1 2 3 4 5 6 7 8 9 1 0 DOC DOC 0 9 8 7 6 5

Library of Congress Cataloging-in-Publication Data
Hounsome, Drayson.
  The baffled parent's guide to coaching girls' soccer / Drayson Hounsome. — 1st U.S. ed.
    p.   cm. — (The baffled parent's guides)
  Includes index.
   ISBN 0-07-144092-5 (alk. paper)
  1. Soccer for women — Coaching. 2. Soccer for children — Coaching I. Title. II. Series.
  GV943.8.H68 2005
  796.334'083'42 — dc22   2005003601

Questions regarding the content of this book should be addressed to
Ragged Mountain Press/McGraw-Hill
P.O. Box 220
Camden, ME 04843
www.raggedmountainpress.com

Questions regarding the ordering of this book should be addressed to
The McGraw-Hill Companies
Customer Service Department
P.O. Box 547
Blacklick, OH 43004
Retail customers: 1-800-262-4729
Bookstores: 1-800-722-4726

Contents

Part Two
Exercises and Games: Foundations for the Growth of Players and Coaches

Preface

When I was growing up in Jersey (the Island of Jersey, that is—not New Jersey), the dream of every young boy was to be a professional football player. We played footy every day before school, during morning break, during lunch break, and after school. We played every kind of footy game imaginable: wembley, four-on-four, heads and volleys, 11-on-11, three and in. During break time there would be different footy games going on at the same time with trash cans and bags spread all around the school yard as goals.

We weren't allowed to bring real leather footballs to school in case the windows got smashed, so we used plastic or rubber balls instead. When these ended up on the roof of the science building, which was more often than not, somebody would pull out a tennis ball from his bag, and the game continued. If the tennis ball vanished down the drain, landed on the roof of the science building, or was confiscated for hitting the teacher on schoolyard duty, then we would just stamp on a soda can and use that. Whenever the custodian would throw down all the balls from the roof, there would be a huge cheer and a sudden mad rush to claim the best ball for your game!

Since realizing my schoolyard dream of being a famous footy player and playing for Nottingham Forest was just that . . . a dream, I've been lucky enough to do the next best thing.

For the past 12 years I've been coaching soccer at levels ranging from 4-year-old beginners to professional players. I've gained advanced coaching licenses from the United States Soccer Federation (USSF), the National Soccer Coaches Association of America (NSCAA), and the English Football Association (F.A) and hold a Bachelor of Science degree with honors in Sport Science and Physical Education from England's premier sporting institute, Loughborough University.

For 10 years I've had the privilege of working for Noga Soccer, one of the largest and most respected private soccer education companies in the country, and have had the opportunity to work alongside and learn from many talented and successful coaches from all over the world. During this time I've developed and implemented a range of coaching programs for youth soccer clubs, lectured on soccer at the university level, and conducted a wide variety of coaching and educational clinics for both experienced and novice coaches. I've been fortunate to coach and train some of the best girls' youth soccer teams in the region, including four different New York state championship teams and have also been part of the Eastern New York Soccer Association (NYSA) girls' Olympic Development Program.

I've been coaching women's soccer at the collegiate level since 1996, the last 4 years as head coach at the CW Post Campus of Long Island University. In 2003 the team won the NCAA Division II ECAC Championship for the first time in the program's history.

Whether you're a professional soccer player scoring goals for Man-

Coach Hounsome gives
pregame instructions.

chester United, a collegiate player winning NCAA championships with
North Carolina, or a 5-year-old playing three-on-three for the first time, the
game of soccer has something magical to offer. Soccer has been part of my
life for as long as I can remember, and it's a great pleasure to be able to pass
on my coaching knowledge, experience, ideas, and insights through this
book.

Introduction

Soccer is by far the most popular sport on the planet. A record number of girls and women are playing soccer worldwide. In the United States the number of female participants has risen from 7.5 million in 1998 to almost 9 million in 2002. The number of universities and colleges in the NCAA that sponsor women's soccer has increased 40-fold in the last 27 years and risen to an all-time high with 879 programs.

Women's soccer in the United States leads the world. In 1999 the USA national team won the World Cup in front of 90,000 spectators in Pasadena, California, making household names out of stars like Mia Hamm and Brandi Chastain. A professional women's soccer league was established, providing youth players and fans the ability to live and breathe the game like never before.

The enormous popularity has led to a dramatic increase in the number of opportunities available for girls to participate in organized soccer at every level, from middle school to high school to youth soccer leagues. This huge growth in girls' soccer means there's a need for more and more parents to step up and volunteer themselves as coaches. Which is where you fit in.

If you've never coached before, or never even played soccer for that matter, don't worry. Whether you're a first-time coach or one who's been coaching for several years, *Coaching Girls' Soccer: The Baffled Parent's Guide* is here to help you. This book will guide, teach, inform, and lead you in the right direction to becoming a successful girls' soccer coach. Success, to me, is not measured in wins and losses but in the number of girls given the opportunity to learn the world's greatest game and experience the love, teamwork, social interaction, sportsmanship, and fun of playing sports.

Coaching Girls' Soccer: The Baffled Parent's Guide is designed to help all parents and coaches who work with girls up to the age of 13 become better and more informed coaches and educators.

With girls playing soccer at an increasingly younger age, there's a need to learn and understand how to teach the game to very young children. The book provides teaching techniques, ideas, modifications, and adventure games for beginners from the age of 4 and provides new coaches with the basic rules of soccer and how they should be adapted for the age of your players.

This book highlights the important differences that exist between girls and boys and discusses the many issues faced by girls' coaches. Part One helps both novice and experienced coach develop teaching and organizational skills and offers insight into coaching techniques that are vital to motivate and build confidence in girls. It runs through each of the essential techniques needed to play soccer, from dribbling to shooting. I've identified how to teach each skill successfully to girls in order to provide maximum repetition and development, provided key coaching points, and outlined many common mistakes and tips for avoiding them.

The most specialized position and therefore possibly the least coached position is that of goalkeeper. This book covers the essential techniques needed for all goalkeepers so that, at long last, your keepers can get the teaching and coaching they need.

You'll learn how to teach essential tactics and soccer strategies to your girls during practice and show them how to successfully attack, defend, and keep possession as a team. There's practical advice on how to plan, organize, and run a session from soup to nuts and a structured format for all your practices. I'll lead you through the process of managing and coaching an entire season and teach you how to successfully coach girls during a game.

Throughout the book there's reference to a myriad of original games and practices. The games are numbered consecutively from 1 to 84. Each game and exercise comes with a detailed description in Part Two, and many include suggested progressions and a diagram. Although there's a suggested age for each exercise, the level of difficulty can be modified to meet the actual ability of your group of players. These games and exercises will provide you with a wide resource of activities, so that you can step onto the field with the knowledge that you're ready to teach any aspect of soccer to your team.

PART ONE

Coaching 101: Everything You Need to Know about Coaching Girls' Soccer

CHAPTER 1

What's Different in Coaching Girls' Soccer?

What makes coaching girls' soccer, you ask, different from coaching boys' soccer? Is it like lacrosse, where the rules are different? Do I need to coach differently with girls? Are there any special qualifications for coaching girls? Are girls easier or harder to coach than boys? Should the coach push girls as hard as boys? What are the differences in motivating girls? What techniques and approaches should I adopt when coaching girls? Do boys and girls grow differently?

There are many questions you might be asking yourself about coaching girls' soccer. This chapter will give you some answers to these many questions.

Girls' Soccer vs. Boys' Soccer

It's important to know that girls' soccer is no different from boys' soccer. Unlike some sports where the rules are different for males and females, in soccer they are identical; the rules, equipment, duration of the game, goal size—everything's the same. There are no special qualifications required to coach girls' soccer. The technical, tactical, mental, and physical demands of the game are the same whether for boys or girls. The techniques and tactics that need to be mastered to be able to play successfully are the same and should therefore be coached at the same level with the same expectations. Girls can and should be pushed as hard as boys.

Some consider girls' soccer to be easier to coach than boys' soccer, but for me both have their challenges. Many coaches prefer to coach girls because they feel that girls have a willingness to be coached and are keen to learn and find out what the coach knows. Girls have a tendency to be more cerebral and group oriented than boys, providing the coach with a highly rewarding coaching experience.

Physiological Differences

Not too long ago young girls were discouraged from participating in sports as it was not considered feminine to develop athletic physiques or to display physical aggression in athletic competition. In today's society, however, with changing attitudes and ever growing media coverage of women's sports on television, girls are being encouraged at a younger age to participate in athletic competition, and consequently many of the differences in athletic accomplishments between boys and girls are fading away.

Prior to puberty there are very few physiological differences between boys and girls, and it's common for young soccer teams to be co-ed. As young girls tend to be physically less aggressive toward each other compared with boys, they need to be encouraged to be more physical in their game. They need to know that it's OK to be physical and play tough, and they should be encouraged to dive into headers, make tackles, and generally be as physical as they can within the rules of the game. With the onset of puberty, girls and boys go through many changes. Girls experience puberty as a sequence of events, with these pubertal changes usually beginning on average 2 years before boys. Girls tend to reach puberty at around 8 to 13 years whereas boys go through puberty at around 9½ to 14. One of the many changes that take place is increased hormone production by the body. Testosterone is produced in greater amounts in boys, while estrogen is produced in greater quantities in girls. This results in boys developing more muscle mass per unit volume of body mass than girls do and increased levels of aggression. Girls increase not only in height and weight but also in body fat and body shape. In both sexes there is a change in size, with the feet, arms, legs, and hands all beginning to grow in advance of the body.

So while puberty leads to boys developing into stronger, faster, and more aggressive players, girls are forced to deal with a rapidly changing body that's not as strong, as fast, or as aggressive. Techniques that girls mastered previously may not seem so natural or easy to them anymore, and many will have to relearn skills with their "new" body. It's important that great patience is shown over this time period and that players understand it's very normal to go through this process.

The onset and rate of puberty vary from player to player so those individuals who reach puberty earlier or later than their peers will often become self-conscious about their bodies. It's vital for the coach to be sympathetic and caring to those who might be embarrassed, and to continue to build the girls' self-esteem through a positive coaching environment.

A key pubertal change in girls around the age of 10 to 16 is the start of the menstrual cycle. This will cause both emotional and physical changes in the players that you should be aware of such as headaches, cramping, and water retention. This is obviously a very sensitive issue and should be handled with a great deal of care and compassion.

Coaching Advice

"If a player complains that she doesn't feel well, encourage her to continue playing, but let her know that it's fine for her to rest and sit out if she feels she needs to. If a female athlete is to continue to participate in sports as she gets older, it's important for her to learn how to play and participate during the menstrual cycle."

Psychological Differences

Prior to puberty there are very few psychological differences between boys and girls; they both play soccer to have fun, to compete, and to interact socially. With puberty, girls become more group and relationship oriented than boys. One of the primary reasons they play soccer is the desire to be part of a team, participate as one of a group of players, and gain satisfaction from the relationships and friendships they build.

The relationship they build with the coach is unique and must be preserved. By consistently showing confidence in and respect for each girl, you'll create a strong and durable relationship with them. Even if you're unhappy with a particular girl's play, it's important to let her know that this has not affected your view of her as a person or your relationship with her. Girls need to know that you care for them above and beyond their abilities as soccer players. If girls get a sense that their relationship with you is dependent on their success on the field, it won't be a close and effective coaching relationship.

If this relationship is destroyed by criticizing players in public or not speaking with them after a game, you'll be faced with difficulty in motivating them and building their confidence. Try not to criticize girls as a result of temporary or present limitations—it's never beneficial; always think about a player's potential ability. The coach who starts moaning at the players and criticizing them over mistakes during a game is far more likely to lose the game than the coach who remains positive and compliments good play throughout.

As a coach of girls, you'll need to pay close attention to the social dynamics of the team. From an early age girls show more psychological aggression toward each other and are more likely to develop cliques and attempt to exclude individuals than do boys. It's important to observe the group closely and attempt to understand what social forces, if any, may be limiting their progress. Care must be taken to encourage inclusion of everybody, by frequently assigning different partners and groups to work with. Girls are unable to function as a team if the players don't get along as individuals, so it's vital to prevent cliques from forming. With boys this is less of an issue, as they find it much easier to temporarily forget about any differences they may have with teammates during game time.

Motivational Differences

Another difference between girls and boys is how they are motivated. Girls tend to be motivated by pleasing others, whereas boys tend to be motivated largely by personal gratification, the "me" mentality.

Girls are motivated by knowing how their efforts affect the results of the team and the performance of their teammates. It's important for them to know that you recognize their efforts. They're motivated by you showing and having confidence in their ability. By giving players your confidence, you'll

---

Coaching Advice

"When a girl hasn't played well, make an extra effort once she steps off the field to engage her in conversation that has nothing to do with soccer."

Coaching Advice

"Try to prevent the same four or five girls from always being on the same team by continuously making girls work with different partners and in different groups. This is an important way to control the power dynamics within the team."

Push girls as hard as you can by creating an environment that is competitive, challenging, and fun.

build theirs. Always let them know when you're pleased with them; don't assume that they know you're happy. Encourage and praise small successes and look for positive signs of progress. Every player on your team has something to contribute, and it's your job as the coach to find and develop each girl's strength. Try to highlight all contributions—physical, emotional, and mental.

Girls place a high value on what others think of them and how they fit into a group. As a result, they find it very tough competing against their friends in practice. They're great competing against other teams but will try to avoid direct competition with their friends. In order to create intensity in practice, however, it's vital that players do compete against each other. Teaching them and getting them to do this is one of the greatest challenges you'll face as a girls' soccer coach.

Performance Differences

Prior to puberty, no significant differences in performance exist between boys and girls. With puberty and the changes that take place, differences in performance do become evident.

With higher levels of testosterone and more muscle mass, male soccer players have increased physical strength. It means that they're faster and stronger and are able to pass and strike the ball harder and over greater distances than females. Goalkeepers are able to jump higher and kick farther. By the time players are in their early teens, it's very evident that with boys' increased strength and power, their game has become much faster and more physical than the girls' game. Speed of play, decision making, and technical

Coaching Advice

"Explain to girls that by pushing their teammates as hard as they can in practice and by competing as hard as they can against each other, they're actually helping each other improve and become stronger players."

preparation all become quicker for boys. Very often, however, these abilities don't become quick enough, and the game becomes too fast for the technical and tactical ability of the players, leading to a breakdown in performance.

Tactical implications in the women's game, with more teams playing with three forwards and playing a higher-pressure game, have helped to increase the overall speed of play. With a faster women's game at the highest level over recent years, it's vital to create a practice environment where girls are continuously forced to make quicker decisions and play technically faster.

To overcome some of the difficulties encountered with playing passes over long distances (40–60 yards) and striking the ball hard, girls must be coached to become highly proficient at short- to mid-range passing (20–40 yards), switching the play at speed (i.e., quickly moving the ball from one side of the field to the other), and shooting with a high degree of accuracy. All players, but goalkeepers in particular, must be encouraged to develop and improve leg strength and vertical jumping ability.

CHAPTER 2

Issues with Coaching Girls

The increased participation in sports by girls has led to an increase in the number of instances and reports of serious issues that every girls' coach must be aware of. Coaches need to understand, know how to deal with, and know how to prevent issues such as eating disorders, sexual harassment, and injuries. This chapter examines these coaching issues and discusses what can be done to prevent them from occurring.

Sexual Harassment

Any coach dealing with young children, regardless of gender, needs to be aware of what can be deemed sexual harassment. Obviously a male coach working with young girls should be highly vigilant and aware of potential situations that may be considered harassment.

Sexual harassment can be defined as any unwelcome sexual advances, requests for sexual favors, or any verbal or physical conduct that creates a sexually hostile environment.

You must be aware that treating a girl in any manner that could be potentially offensive or intimidate her, regardless of intent, may be deemed as sexual harassment. Some actions that could lead to a sexually hostile environment are sexual jokes, improper language, sexual conversations, rating of girls, improper touching, or "catcalls."

As the coach you are responsible for player supervision throughout practice.

Coaching Advice

"When setting up your practice area, also set up a small area off to the side as your base camp. This should be at least 10 yards away from where you're going to practice. This is the area where the girls keep their bags and drinks, and where any equipment and extra soccer balls that aren't being used should be kept. Avoid setting up bags and drinks on nearby bleachers, as this is a potentially dangerous situation where young players could climb up and fall off the moment your back is turned."

Even if your actions have no sexual intent, use common sense and avoid the following situations or potential problems that could lead to accusations of sexual harassment:

- Never allow yourself to be alone with a child
- If a player is waiting for a ride after practice, ask for an additional parent to wait with you
- Don't interact with players in social activities that are not team related
- Don't use foul or suggestive language toward any player
- Don't make phone calls or send e-mails that could be considered questionable in any manner

What may be innocent to you may be interpreted as sexual harassment in the courts of law, so always be overly cautious.

Legal Issues

Anyone who's working with children is responsible for the children they're supervising. In today's lawsuit-happy world, it's important to avoid any problems or dangerous situations that could result in legal problems.

Supervise players at all times. If you leave the field to go to the restroom and an injury occurs, you could be held liable. You should select a parent for every practice who must stay at the field or find an assistant coach to help with supervision. If you leave a practice early and the team is left alone, you're also liable if any problems occur.

Before every practice check the playing area for items that could cause injury, such as needles, broken glass, rocks, or holes. Ensure that unused balls and equipment are out of the way and off the playing area. If someone gets injured by tripping over a ball net, you could be found liable.

If you always remember that the safety of all players is your responsibility from the start of practice until the time they are collected from the field, and if you act accordingly, you'll ensure potential problems with legal issues are avoided.

Soccer Injuries

Although injury rates in soccer players are low compared with other sports, minor injuries do occur. As soccer is a contact sport with quick turns, the most common injuries occur with the knees, ankles, and feet. Most are caused by either a single twist or blow or by a buildup of stress to a joint or tendon over time. Common injuries include bruises, sprains, strains, and cuts and can be dealt with mostly by you.

Although the risk of serious injuries is rare with young girls, the seriousness of injuries does increase with age and the level of competition.

Coaching Advice

"Whenever a girl gets injured in practice or in a game, it's good habit to get the remaining players to sit or kneel on your command, so as to avoid further injuries while you're dealing with the injured player."

RICE for Minor Injuries

Many minor injuries occur from a collision or twist and lead to some swelling of the injured body part. If a girl receives a soft-tissue injury, commonly known as a sprain or a strain, the best immediate treatment is RICE (Rest, Ice, Compression, and Elevation).

Rest. Move the player to the side of the field if she's unable to get there on her own. She should rest the injured body part for at least 48 hours.

Ice. Apply ice indirectly to the swollen area for 20 minutes every hour. Use a cold pack, an ice bag, or a plastic bag filled with crushed ice that's been wrapped in a towel. Wrapping the ice in a bag or towel is essential to avoid skin or nerve damage.

Compression. Add compression by wrapping an elastic bandage around the injured area. This will help reduce swelling and promote faster healing.

Elevation. Elevate the injured area as high above the heart as is comfortable. Gravity will help to reduce fluid flow to the area and reduce swelling.

Applying RICE as soon as possible after the injury occurs and applying all the components at the same time ensures that swelling is reduced quickly and promotes a fast recovery.

Most serious injuries can be avoided with age-appropriate practices and by maintaining a fairly even competitive level. A less-developed child competing against a mature child is at a greater risk of injury, so players should be matched up and grouped according to skill level, weight, and physical maturity. Obviously, practicing heading from goalkeeper punts with 8-year-olds is an inappropriate practice that could lead to serious injury.

When dealing with a possible severe injury, assess immediately whether it's life threatening. Any back, head, or neck injury should be considered severe, and you should call emergency services immediately. If you're unsure of what's injured, ask the girl where it hurts. If you sense something is broken, keep the area immobile. This may involve not moving the girl at all.

Most injuries you'll see aren't severe, and although it's actually very unlikely that you'll have to deal with a severe injury at all, you must still have an emergency plan in case it should occur. Basic first-aid and CPR training are highly recommended.

Before your first practice be sure you have a first-aid kit to deal with any minor injuries. Your first-aid kit should include the following items:

- Cleansing wipes
- Bandages
- Ice packs
- Sterile gloves
- First-aid tape
- Elastic bandages
- Safety pins

Sprains and Strains

A sprain is an injury to a ligament, whereas a strain is an injury to either a muscle or a tendon. A ligament is a band of tough, fibrous tissue that connects two or more bones at a joint and prevents excessive movement of the joint. When there's a sprain, one or more ligaments can be injured at the same time. Muscles are bundles of specialized cells that contract when stimulated and produce movement. Tendons are the tough, fibrous cords of tissue that connect muscles to bones.

During the summer months always remember to carry sunscreen—just in case the parents have forgotten. Sun protection will decrease the chances of potentially deadly skin cancer that can occur later in life.

Female Athlete Triad

As girls reach an age where appearance and body image become very important to them, a syndrome known as the *female athlete triad* may begin to develop. This could be in girls as young as 8 to 13 years old. The female athlete triad is a syndrome that occurs almost exclusively in physically active girls and women. It involves three interrelated components: eating disorders, amenorrhea, and osteoporosis. Individuals who exhibit symptoms of one part of the triad are at a significantly increased risk to experience the others. Each component or a combination of the three can severely decrease physical performance and health into adulthood and can even lead to death.

Although it's evident mostly in teens and young women, the seeds for the triad are often developed at a much earlier age. As a coach working with physically active young girls, you should be familiar with the issues surrounding female athlete triad. By educating parents and creating an awareness of the warning signs, early detection and intervention can take place.

Eating Disorders

The first component of the triad, eating disorders, affects a high number of female athletes. The eating disorder is such that a girl's food intake does not provide enough calories to cover the needs of her activities and training. It's important to understand that this doesn't have to be a conscious restriction of caloric intake and can result from a poor family diet or irregular meal pattern.

Anorexia and bulimia are the most talked-about disorders and can result from a variety of causes, such as a father suggesting to his daughter that her soccer performance would improve if she lost a few pounds. In both conditions the girls don't get the proper nutrition and suffer both physical and emotional problems. With anorexia, girls literally starve themselves, while with bulimia they overeat initially and then attempt to get rid of the calories they've consumed through intentional vomiting and excessive exercise.

Amenorrhea

The second component, amenorrhea, occurs when the menstrual cycle is dysfunctional. A caloric deficit resulting from eating disorders and excessive exercise leaves too little energy to maintain the endocrine reproductive system, and so the menstrual cycle stops. Long periods of amenorrhea can lead to severe health-related issues. Once again, educating parents about the signs of amenorrhea, such as compulsive over-exercise and irregular menstrual cycle, can help lead to early intervention. It's important to be concerned about amenorrhea, as it's highly correlated with osteoporosis, the final component of the triad.

Osteoporosis

Osteoporosis is a decrease in bone density and traditionally develops later in a woman's life. Premature bone loss or inadequate bone formation results in low bone mass, micro architectural deterioration, increased skeletal fragility, and an increased risk of stress fractures. It's vital for young female soccer players to build their bone mass during their teenage years and in their 20s, through a balanced diet rich in calcium and vitamin D. If athletes don't develop optimal bone density and are losing bone mass when it should be forming, then they'll suffer from premature and irreversible osteoporosis.

By looking for the following predisposing risk factors and by educating both players and parents about nutrition and dietary needs, you can help prevent the onset and development of the female athlete triad:

• Chronic weight fluctuations and dieting
• Low self-esteem
• Family dysfunction
• Poor nutrition
• Traumatic events
• Pressure to lose weight from parents, coaches, and peers
• Over-emphasis on body weight for performance
• Excessive physical training

Nutrition

Young female soccer players need a lot of nutrients to fuel their growing bodies, so educating parents about the importance of eating a well-balanced and nutritional diet is essential. Although it's widely known that nutrition is a vital part of good health, it's still common for young girls to eat junk food, skip meals, and eat the same kinds of food day after day. Parents must understand that poor eating habits lead to a lack of nutrients in the diet, which impairs both growth and performance. As outlined earlier, failure to meet the nutritional needs of girls when they enter puberty can lead to severe health consequences.

To follow a healthy diet, encourage and explain to the parents of your players the following nutritional principles.

Variety: As no single food contains all the nutrients your players need for optimum health, growth, and performance, they must eat a variety of foods daily from each food group, as well as different foods from within each group.

Moderation: To avoid eating too little or too much of any one food, players should eat each food in moderation.

Balance: The caloric (energy) intake and the energy expended must be balanced to maintain a healthy weight and body composition. Without sufficient calories a player will feel weak and fatigued, and her athletic performance may suffer. To increase caloric intake, players should eat carbohydrates such as potatoes, rice, pasta, beans, and bread. Complex carbohydrates are an excellent source of energy for soccer.

The most appropriate diet for the girls on your soccer team is one that is high in nutrient-dense complex carbohydrates; one that is low in fat, saturated fat, and cholesterol; and one that contains a moderate amount of protein. They should not worry about eating more protein as simply increasing caloric intake in a well-balanced diet will provide the extra protein that they require.

In addition to a well-balanced and nutritional diet, your players must consume additional fluids to replace those lost through exercise and playing soccer. To prevent dehydration and overheating, the girls should drink plenty of water or sports drink before practicing and then drink again every 15 to 20 minutes during the practices and games. It's important they take on additional fluids even if they're not thirsty. How much each girl should drink can vary widely, depending on age, size, build, level of activity, and also the weather. These daily requirements generally range from 1 to 1½ pints for 4- to 8-year-olds and from 2½ to 4 pints for 9- to 12-year-olds, with an additional 8 to 12 ounces of fluid needed for every half hour of soccer.

CHAPTER 3

Developing a Learning Environment

One of the most significant things you must do as the coach is develop an environment where girls feel comfortable with their surroundings. They must feel comfortable with you, their teammates, and the environment in which they're learning. This chapter will show you how to create a fun and enjoyable soccer environment, by maximizing learning opportunities and player development, and what to avoid.

Make It Fun

Girls want to play soccer because it's fun. If girls aren't having fun, they'll almost definitely not stay with the team and may even leave the game of soccer all together. Therefore it's up to you, the coach, to make it fun. Creating a fun atmosphere at practice increases the enjoyment of all the players, enhancing the learning process.

Having fun means different things to different people. The ability to perform skills successfully and accomplish challenges brings a high degree of satisfaction and enjoyment for most. Setting both individual and group challenges throughout practice helps create this fun learning environment.

The manner in which the coach sets up every practice and game often determines the level of fun that can be derived from it. I've observed, for example, many coaches who instruct players at the start of practice to "go and juggle." Very often the girls go off in small groups and chat, as they simply don't have fun "just" juggling.

To make juggling fun, as with all aspects of soccer, it must be challenging and rewarding. If at the start of every practice you ask the players to see how many juggles they can do in, say, 3 minutes with just their feet, you'll see them become excited by the challenge very quickly. If you ask them weekly to improve their own personal juggling best and keep a record of how they've done, they'll not only work hard for these 3 minutes, but on seeing measurable improvement over time, they'll receive satisfaction and enjoyment from the activity. I've observed many groups of girls become absolute juggling fanatics when exposed to the activity in this manner.

Girls derive enjoyment and fun from playing games and activities that challenge them, so it's important that all are involved as often as possible, with very few periods of inactivity. A common mistake with many novice coaches is that they frequently play games where players are eliminated. If a girl is eliminated and becomes inactive, she may no longer feel involved with the game. This can lead to a reduction in both enjoyment and overall soccer development.

A common elimination game is where all the girls dribble around and attempt to kick each other's soccer balls out of an area while maintaining control of their own. Once a girl's ball is kicked out, she's eliminated, with the winner being the last girl left in. Unfortunately, the girls who need the most practice with ball control are usually eliminated first, so as well as having less fun they're also not able to have the opportunity to improve their ball-control abilities. Games where players are eliminated create a limited learning environment and should be avoided or modified.

Knock Out Five (see Game 10 on page 139) is a simple modification that increases the fun element, reduces periods of inactivity, and improves the overall learning environment. Making the winner the first girl to kick out five soccer balls, instead of the last remaining player, and allowing those who've been kicked out to reenter the game once they've performed five juggles are two examples of how elimination games can be modified.

To keep practices fun and active, avoid spending long periods of time talking to the girls to explain the game or technique you're trying to teach. Explanations should be very brief, with games allowed to develop and progress while being played. Instead of giving all the rules at the start, give just the essential rules and then let the girls play, gradually adding conditions and rules over time. The younger the group, the more important it becomes to give little bite-sized pieces of instruction regarding techniques and rules over the period of a game, as opposed to all at once.

Activities such as drink breaks or collecting cones can also be a fun element of every practice, by once again making it challenging and competitive. For example, a drink break can be quick and fun by making it a challenge. Tell players they must do three headers with the ball, run over to their drinks as fast as they can, have 10 gulps of drink, and then come back and be singing their favorite song to the coach.

Practices must vary from week to week in order to keep the learning environment fun and fresh. Try to avoid repeating the same exercise too often. Simply changing the names of some games or the theme of a game will keep young players interested and excited by your practices.

Be Positive

Girls can never hear enough of "Good job," "Nice try," or "Well done." Everybody loves to hear praise and encouragement, so give it. Positive encouragement is a vital component in a successful learning environment. Girls learn and develop more quickly when immersed in coaching that's positive and supporting. Be a positive coach who's enthusiastic and who's continuously reinforcing good performances. If you're negative and always highlight weaknesses, then many girls will get turned off by your approach and will look to leave your team.

Girls value their relationship with the coach, so always show them how happy you are when you see them perform a technique or activity successfully. If they see you're excited and happy with their performance, they'll try to repeat what they've done to please you. Point out when a girl has performed a technique well. Get her to demonstrate in front of the rest of the group, explaining what she's done to make it so successful. This not only helps to increase the girl's self-esteem but also helps her and the other players understand the correct way to perform the technique.

Feedback Sandwich

To remain positive while correcting girls, try using a well-known technique called the Feedback Sandwich. It involves giving a positive statement first with positive feedback, followed by a corrective statement and then by an overall positive summation.

For example, 9-year-old Christina is working extremely hard in practice, dribbling past defenders and shooting, yet she keeps hitting the ball over the goal. A coach might say: "You're working hard, Christina, but you've got to stop missing the goal. Try to score."

This doesn't help her in any way and will likely only add to her inability to score as her frustration increases. Using the Feedback Sandwich approach, you'd say: "Christina, you're doing a great job beating defenders as you're changing direction with that step over and accelerating into space. When you're about to strike the ball, you're just leaning back, causing the ball to go upward. Try keeping your head down and follow through once you've hit the ball, and it will go on target. You're working so hard. Keep it up."

This provides Christina with plenty of positive reenforcement of what she's doing well and the corrective solution to improve her shooting, all while maintaining a positive learning environment.

Patience

As all girls are different and react to feedback in different manners, it's vital to be continuously positive. By keeping all feedback positive, you'll ensure the girls never feel that they're personally at fault or bad for the mistakes they make.

One key aspect to providing this positive learning environment is the importance of patience. Improvement takes place over time, following from mistakes, so patience is a vital ingredient to successfully coach girls. The coach must remain positive despite the repeated mistakes that are being made. You should let girls know that you recognize they're trying hard and that you have confidence in them and their ability. If you get frustrated and lose your patience with a group of girls, especially if they're trying their best and working hard, it may have a severe impact on the learning environment as they feel they're unable to please you with their performance, no matter how hard they try.

Motivation

Girls need to be motivated at practice in order to create a successful learning environment. Motivation can either be intrinsic or extrinsic. Intrinsic motivation is the drive to do something because of the satisfaction derived internally from doing it, while extrinsic motivation results from an outside source.

Intrinsically motivated individuals are more likely to work harder on their own to improve, and they find considerable enjoyment just from participating. By creating fun and enjoyable practices and by providing a high level of encouragement and positive reinforcement, a coach is going a long way to develop this intrinsic motivation among the players. In addition to having fun practices with positive reinforcement, the coach, by setting goals with girls, can also stimulate this motivation. Both individual and group goals that are challenging but achievable help provide a high degree of motivation.

Discipline

In order to maintain order within the learning environment, a level of discipline is necessary. A set of rules and guidelines is required that outlines what's appropriate and inappropriate behavior for the girls. Learning discipline and responsibility is a great additional benefit received through participation in sport.

When setting your team rules and guidelines, remember to keep them simple and to establish how they'll be enforced. Setting the guidelines for your team isn't necessarily the most difficult aspect of establishing discipline at your practices, but how these rules are enforced certainly is. Different rules will require different methods of enforcement. Failure to enforce these rules ultimately leads to players and parents losing respect for them altogether, resulting in a less disciplined learning environment.

Some essential rules should include punctuality, equipment, and respect. All rules must start at the top, with the coach. As the coach, you must

Coaching Advice

"Instructing a team of girls to juggle for 3 minutes and asking them who will be the first to achieve 50 juggles will motivate only a few of those involved to work hard. It will motivate those players who can get close to achieving this goal of 50 juggles, but it will have a negative effect on those less able who might only be able to reach 10 juggles. They'll be less motivated as this challenge isn't a realistic goal for them. Asking the group to beat their personal highest from a previous week motivates every girl, as it's an achievable goal for all."

Coaching Advice

"The girls rely on their parents to get them everywhere on time. So making a girl run laps because she's late doesn't make the parents any more likely to bring her on time. It only hurts the girl further, as her level of enjoyment is reduced by the punishment. When a girl is repeatedly late, it's important to talk to her parents about the importance of punctuality within a team setting. Explain that by arriving late they're hurting their daughter's soccer development because she's missing key elements at every practice. I've found that if parents are made to realize that they're limiting their daughter's development and that their daughter is falling behind because she's always arriving late, the punctuality soon improves."

lead by example. If the coach is always late or shows no respect to officials or the opposition, then the rules will be impossible to enforce.

Punctuality—girls should arrive on time for practices and games.
Equipment—girls should bring a soccer ball, a drink, shin guards, and cleats to every practice and game.
Respect—girls and parents should treat teammates, opponents, officials, and coaches with the utmost respect. During practice, the girls should show respect for the coach by paying attention at all times and by not talking when the coach is talking.

The importance of respect among teammates is essential for good team chemistry, especially with girls. If respect and team chemistry don't exist, cliques will soon develop, and then certain individuals will be excluded from certain groups. Cliques within any team ultimately create a lot of disharmony. Good team chemistry through discipline and respect is something to pay close attention to at all times when coaching girls.

Practicing outside the Comfort Zone

The biggest challenge for any girls' coach as the players get older and become teenagers is getting them to perform and practice outside their comfort zone. For maximal development and improvement to occur within the learning environment, they must practice at an intensity and level with which they're normally not comfortable. By performing at their technical edge they'll make mistakes executing actions they normally could do with no problems. When practice is performed outside the comfort zone, player development and performance are significantly improved. Competition is the essential element needed for a girl to perform at her technical edge—competition against herself and her teammates.

Girls often have greater difficulty than boys performing outside their comfort zone, as they place a high value on what others think of them and how they fit into the group. They find it very tough competing against their friends in practice and will often try to avoid direct competition. In order to create intensity in practice, however, and to have players perform at their technical edge, it's vital that they do compete against each other. Once you have a team of girls who push and compete against each other 100 percent in practice, and you have players performing outside their comfort zone, then the optimal learning environment is in place.

Soccer for Life

To have a longer-lasting effect on every girl, the coach must create in each girl a love for soccer when off the field and away from practice. Get the girls involved in watching games on television. Take them to high school and college games and get them to choose soccer heroes and role models. By surrounding them and exposing them to soccer, you'll help them develop a true love for the game that goes beyond just playing.

CHAPTER 4

Essential Teaching and Coaching Skills

To be a successful coach and to teach the game to young children you need to know more than just how to play the game. Technical and tactical understanding are essential, but if you're unable to effectively communicate this knowledge, or are unable to efficiently organize a practice, then your vast knowledge will never be passed on to your group of girls. This chapter will teach you the importance of developing good communication skills and the teaching process that must be followed for learning to occur. You'll learn the secrets used by teachers and coaches and the methods used to teach new skills and techniques.

Communication

Effective communication skills are essential to successfully interact with both your players and their parents. You must learn to use both verbal and nonverbal communication skills. Verbal communication is what you say and how you say it. Girls will interpret a lot from how a message is conveyed, so speak clearly, with confidence, in an enthusiastic and encouraging manner. Changing the volume, tone, and speed of your voice will maintain the group's attention while you're speaking. Never use foul or abusive language either to the group or to an individual. Avoid the use of soccer terminology with very young girls and always use language that is age appropriate for understanding. A common mistake with novice coaches is overtalking and taking too long to get the point across. Players simply lose attention, and only segments of the message you're trying to communicate are received. Communicate your point quickly and concisely, and then let the practice continue.

Nonverbal communication is how body language speaks for you. Make direct eye contact with each girl when you speak. This will capture the girls' attention and make them feel important, thus helping to build self-confidence. Smiling when talking can affect greatly how your message is

Coaching Advice

"When talking to your team as a group, don't let them face the sun. They'll be distracted by the sun in their eyes and won't be able to focus on any demonstration or what you're saying."

Coaching Advice

"When your group is spread out across the field and you're communicating information to them, always check by name that the person farthest away can hear you. On a windy day, talk with the wind."

received by the players, as it shows that you're happy and pleased with their efforts. Girls pick up and receive a lot of information from nonverbal communication, so avoid sending unwanted signals and messages to them.

Effective communication is a skill, and there are many ways to improve it. There are books that can be read and courses to attend, but the best way is through making a personal effort at every session to practice different methods of communicating. Try speaking only twice through an entire practice, and let your discovery of communication build from there!

The Teaching Process

When teaching a technique or tactic, you can't just tell the girls what you want them to do and expect that they'll magically be able to do it. There's a logical teaching process that must be followed in order for anything to be mastered.

Step One: Demonstrate. First you must demonstrate the correct action. Trying to simply explain an action in words is complex and often very confusing. Always remember that a picture paints a thousand words. When demonstrating, make the action as realistic as possible, so that the girls can see the final picture of what they're to learn. Demonstrate a technique at game speed and then repeat it slowly, breaking it down into its basic components.

Step Two: Practice Time. Once you've demonstrated an action, give the girls time to practice what you've shown them. They'll make plenty of mistakes, but that's fine. Everybody learns by making mistakes and correcting these mistakes. As the players are practicing, observe and identify what corrective feedback is required.

Step Three: Give Feedback. This feedback can be to either the group or an individual. If there's a common mistake among the girls, it's more efficient to correct the entire team. Highlight no more than two mistakes at a given time and explain what can be done to correct them. Once again, a demonstration may be required. If you've identified a girl who's able to perform the action, use her to demonstrate the correct technique. This is a great way of building self-confidence and also convinces the other players that they, too, can do a particular action. If most of the group is performing the action well, there's no need to stop the entire group. Just stop those who need assistance and let the others continue to work on the action.

While you're observing your players practice, it's important to also give individual feedback. This works to satisfy the girls' need for personal recognition. This feedback can either be corrective or simply reinforce that a girl is performing well. When giving feedback, always remain positive throughout.

Once you've made a correction or positive reinforcement of performance, give the girls time to practice again. This process is repeated until an action is mastered at a certain level. It obviously takes a lot of repetition to master many skills, so you must balance out making corrections and letting the girls play. Once the players have mastered a skill or technique at one level, you must adjust the practices and increase the pressure, challenging the girls to perform at a higher level.

If, for example, you're teaching dribbling moves, adding defenders to the activity will allow the skill mastered with no pressure to be practiced with increased pressure.

Teaching Skills

Freeze Method

When making a correction during a practice, use the Freeze method. On your command of "Freeze," all players must freeze exactly where they are and not move. This is very useful when teaching positioning and correcting decision making, as it allows players to see at that moment exactly where they should be positioned or what options are available. Players can be moved into the correct position before allowing the exercise or game to continue.

Copy the Coach Method

When teaching a new skill or move, play a game called Copy the Coach to demonstrate and teach the fundamentals of the technique. Whatever the coach does, the girls must copy. Spread the group out so that players have plenty of space to perform the technique, yet they're close enough that they can see and hear. If the coach stands on one leg, the players must copy. If the coach jumps up in the air, so must the girls. After several fun and silly Copy the Coach activities, introduce the actual movements you want players to perform. Gradually build up the actions so the technique is eventually performed in one motion.

For example, you can use this method to teach the stop turn by breaking the technique into the following movements for players to copy:

- Stand on one leg
- Scratch your head
- Stretch your arms in the air
- Jog on your toes behind the ball
- Place the sole of your right foot on top of the ball
- Place the sole of your right foot on top of the ball and then jump forward, moving the right foot and upper body sideways beyond the ball
- Place the sole of your right foot on top of the ball and then jump forward, moving the right foot and upper body sideways beyond the ball; bend the right knee and move the left leg over the ball
- Place the sole of your right foot on top of the ball and then jump forward,

Coaching Advice

"If you have very little experience playing soccer and are unable to personally demonstrate an action, an effective picture must still be painted for the players. Break the action down into parts and demonstrate the key individual components slowly, or ask a girl who has already mastered the action at the level being taught to demonstrate for you. Having an assistant coach or older sibling demonstrate an action is also an effective method if you're unable to demonstrate it yourself."

Coaching Advice

"When it comes to personal feedback, I'm a big believer in praising loudly and correcting quietly. If someone is doing an action well, give the positive reinforcement so that all can hear."

moving the right foot and upper body sideways beyond the ball; bend the right knee and move the left leg over the ball; with the outside of the left foot take the ball in the opposite direction

- Place the sole of your right foot on top of the ball and then jump forward, moving the right foot and upper body sideways beyond the ball; bend the right knee and move the left leg over the ball; with the outside of the left foot take the ball in the opposite direction and accelerate away

Organization

An ability to successfully organize will ensure that your sessions and practices run smoothly. Always arrive early and be the first to games and practices. Make a checklist for every practice of what you want to teach and what practices you're going to run. Plan each practice ahead of time in great detail and write down what coaching points you'll try to identify and what games you'll play. Plan additional progressions for those girls who are able to master the techniques ahead of the others. Avoid arriving at the practice 5 minutes late with no idea of what you're going to do.

Developmental Philosophy

To be a successful coach with any youth soccer players, you must focus and place emphasis on individual and team development, rather than on winning at all costs. Soccer is a simple game to play, yet it involves advanced techniques and tactics that need to be mastered in order to play at a higher level. You must stress to the parents and players that success should not be measured by wins but rather by how well each girl learns and develops over time. With a philosophy of player development, your approach to coaching should emphasize the mastering of basic techniques and tactics before developing those that are more advanced.

Stressing player development doesn't mean that winning isn't important. Winning is important (after all, the objective of soccer is to score more goals than your opponent), but it shouldn't be your priority or your primary measure of success.

Concentrating on player development and teaching more advanced actions progressively over time will ensure that your girls are satisfied and motivated by the game and are able to play successfully as they get older and the level of competition increases.

If you measure success with wins and losses, then you'll teach and coach in a manner to ensure that you get those wins. Over time this may prevent players from developing since your focus will be on tactics that bring wins rather than on developing well-rounded soccer players.

CHAPTER 5

How to Play Soccer

When we were kids, every break between classes we would play football—or soccer, as it's known here in the United States. We'd use two trash cans to create one goal at one end of the playground and two bags at the other end of the playground. If there were 10 of us who wanted to play, we'd pick teams from those who were there. If somebody else wanted to play, they'd go find another player, and then each player would go on a team. If we had an odd number at the start, the team without the extra player would have a monkey goalie, whereby the keeper is allowed to play out of goal.

The great thing about soccer is that the game is simple, with very few rules. The rules can be modified to fit the situation, space available, and age of the players. The objective is to score more goals than the other team. A goal is scored by getting the ball over the goal line between the goal posts. Players can use any part of their body except the arms and hands to move the ball up the field and score. The exception to this is the player designated as the goalkeeper. Each team has a goalkeeper who is able to use her hands inside a special area in front of the goal known as the penalty area.

As the coach, you must have a good understanding of the official rules of soccer. However, avoid getting sidetracked and spending endless amounts of time going over rules such as offsides and indirect free kicks with young girls. It's more important for them to spend time with the ball and have fun, so let the games flow. If you currently know nothing about the rules of soccer, this chapter will give you a good start. It'll give you an understanding of the official rules of the game and will also describe many of the adaptations that are used and recommended with younger players.

The Playing Area

The Field

The soccer field is rectangular in shape, with a full-sized field ranging in length from 100 yards to 130 yards and the width ranging from 50 yards to

100 yards. At the end of the field is the goal line, and at the side of the field is the sideline. In the middle of the field is the halfway line or center line. These lines are part of the playing area. (See recommended field sizes for younger players on page 29.)

The Goal

On each goal line is the goal. A full-sized goal is 24 feet wide and 8 feet high. (See recommended sizes for younger players on page 29.)

The Penalty Area

In front of each goal is the penalty area, which extends out 18 yards from each goal post and 18 yards from the goal line. This is the designated area of the field where the goalkeeper can use her hands. Due to its dimensions, the penalty area is also known as the 18-yard box.

The 6-Yard Area

Within the penalty area and directly in front of the goal is a smaller area, extending 6 yards from each goal post and 6 yards from the goal line. This is the area from which all goal kicks are taken.

Modifications

Field Size

With fewer players on the field in younger age groups, the dimensions of the field change. A four-on-four field is smaller than an 11-on-11 field. The field size is generally determined by your club or league and will vary based on the age of the teams and the availability of space. When setting up your fields for practices or games, base the size on the guidelines given in the accompanying table from US Youth Soccer.

Number of Players and Duration of Game

The adult version of soccer (and that played at the professional and collegiate level) is

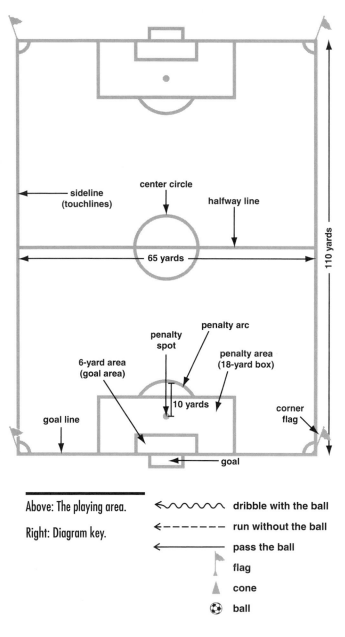

Above: The playing area.

Right: Diagram key.

Age	No. of Players	Field Size	Goal Size	Game Duration
Under 6	3-on-3	25 yd. x 20 yd.	4 ft. x 6 ft.	Four 8-minute periods
Under 8	4-on-4	50 yd. x 30 yd.	6 ft. x 12 ft.	Four 12-minute periods
Under 10	6-on-6	50 yd. x 40 yd.	6 ft. x 12 ft.	Two 25-minute periods
Under 12	8-on-8	70 yd. x 50 yd.	7 ft. x 21 ft.	Two 30-minute periods
12 and over	11-on-11	100 yd. x 70 yd.	8 ft. x 24 ft.	Two 45-minute periods

played with 11 players on one team competing against 11 players on another team. Children are not mini-adults, so with players under the age of 13 this number is totally inappropriate. With fewer players on the field, each girl is given more touches of the ball, more opportunities to pass and shoot, and more opportunities to make decisions, leading to a greater involvement in the game. This fun and faster learning environment develops a more complete player.

Your club, league, or association will decide how many players are on each team. The youngest age groups generally have the fewest number of girls on the field. The accompanying table provides US Youth Soccer's recommendations for the number of player at various ages.

Most girls will want to play and just keep on playing, but official games must have a time restriction so that the game can have an outcome. The adult version of soccer is played for a total of 90 minutes. The game is split into two 45-minute periods, with a short 10-minute break in between. At the youth level, the length of the game varies with age, and this varies between leagues and associations. Most will follow the format recommended by US Youth Soccer as given in the accompanying table.

Player Equipment

One of the great things about soccer is that little equipment is needed to play the game, and the basic equipment that is needed is relatively inexpensive. Each girl should have the following equipment.

Soccer Cleats

Girls aged 4 to 6 can basically play in any kind of athletic shoe, but once they begin to run a bit faster and change direction, more grip is needed, and so soccer cleats are recommended. Because children outgrow their shoes every 6–12 months, don't spend a lot of money on soccer cleats—just buy a basic pair. To avoid injuries, check the size every 6 months and make sure the shoes are still the right fit. Leather cleats are obviously considered the best (kangaroo leather to be exact!), but cleats made of synthetic materials are fine. I want to emphasize the importance of choosing a cleat that fits correctly rather than one that is soft leather or more expensive than another. There is very little need for

It's important to give your girls plenty of drink breaks.

parents to spend a lot of money on expensive cleats for players aged 4–12.

Shin Guards

Soccer is a kicking sport, so when two players go to kick the ball there's a good chance someone will be kicked in the leg. To avoid soft-tissue injuries and fractures of the lower leg, it's vital that every girl wears shin guards. Shin guards are worn on the front of the shin and should be covered by the soccer sock.

Water Bottle

A child's thermo-regulatory system is less developed than that of adults, leaving them more vulnerable to dehydration and the dangers of heat-related illness. Even in cold weather it's important that the girls take drink breaks on a regular basis. Each player should drink approximately 5 to 9 ounces of water or sports drink every 20 minutes. (See the section on Nutrition on page 16 for recommended daily intake of fluids.)

Soccer Ball

In order to maximize player development, it's important that every girl spends as much time with the ball and gets as many opportunities to touch the ball with her feet as possible. The more touches of the ball each girl has, the more she'll develop over time. Time with the ball is maximized if each girl brings her own soccer ball to practice. She'll also need the ball at home for practicing. Each ball should be labeled with the girl's name in permanent ink.

When buying a soccer ball you have a wide range to choose from. All soccer balls today are made of synthetic leather. Lower-end practice balls are usually made from polyvinyl chloride or rubber while more expensive balls are made with polyurethane leather. Soccer balls where the panels are stitched together are of higher quality than those that are glued. Those that are hand stitched are generally the most expensive; those that are machine stitched cost less. No matter what the quality of the soccer ball, always make sure it is the right size and at the recommended pressure. As a general rule add enough air so that the surface of the ball can be pressed in approximately half an inch by the thumbs.

Age	Recommended Soccer Ball Sizes
Under 8	Size #3
Under 12	Size #4
12 and over	Size #5

In general, the younger the girl, the smaller the foot size, so the smaller the ball that should be used. The table opposite provides sizes of soccer balls for each age group as recommended by US Youth Soccer.

Additional Equipment

To keep shin guards in place and in the correct position to protect the lower leg, soccer socks must be worn. These socks should be pulled up over the shin guards at all times. Some leagues or associations require goalkeepers to wear head protectors or mouth guards during games, so check with your club on these rules. If this is a requirement, encourage your goalkeepers to also use this equipment during practice. To avoid jewelry getting caught in hair or jerseys, and causing potential injuries, have your players remove any earrings, bracelets, or necklaces before practice. If you have a player that wears eyeglasses, avoid potential injuries by encouraging her parents to purchase sports goggles for her to wear.

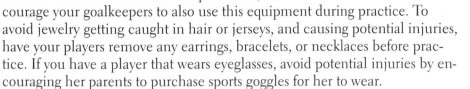

Sports goggles should be worn in place of regular eyeglasses.

Team Equipment

Little equipment is needed for the team as well. Balls, of course, are essential. Some leagues or clubs will provide balls, but they usually don't supply enough for the entire team, so it's best if every girl can bring her own ball to every game and practice. (See the Soccer Ball section opposite.) This will save you carrying loads of soccer balls around, but it's still a good idea to bring two or three extra balls in case one gets lost or is forgotten at home. The table below suggests what to bring to every game and practice. Additional items that are beneficial but not essential include flags and small portable goals.

And what about you? You're a coach, so dress like a coach. It'll be very difficult to demonstrate an action if you're still wearing the suit and tie or the

Item	Quantity
Cones or disks to mark practice areas and goals	16+
Practice vests (bibs or pinnies) to identify different teams	8+
Extra soccer balls to replace forgotten or lost balls	3+
Ball pump with needle to add air to underinflated balls	1
First-aid kit to deal with minor injuries	1
Whistle for refereeing small practice games	1
Watch for ensuring good timing at practice	1

dress you wore to work. Wear good sneakers, cleats if you have them, shorts or training pants, and a T-shirt or sweatshirt. Avoid wearing sunglasses, which prevent you from communicating with your eyes. Nonverbal communication is essential with girls.

Rules of the Game

Prior to competitive travel soccer, keep the rules to a minimum. If you play in a league where there's no offside rule (see pages 36–38), don't complicate the game and confuse your players. Remember to keep it simple. The rules of soccer were developed for the adult game, so it's important when practicing that rules are modified to suit the age and ability of your girls. An example of this is to allow kick-ins instead of throw-ins and to allow the ball to be dribbled into play instead of goal kicks.

Starting the Game

The game officially begins with the kickoff. A coin toss is used to decide which team will take the initial kickoff. The ball is placed in the middle of the field, with each team spread out on their side of the halfway line. The girl taking the kickoff must play the ball forward into the opponent's half of the field. The ball is not considered to be in play (and the game started) until it's traveled one rotation. The girl taking the kickoff cannot touch the ball again until it has been touched by another player, so a second girl must be involved in the kickoff. At the kickoff no players from the opposing team are allowed within 10 yards of the ball.

Once the ball has traveled forward one rotation, it's very common for the second player to retain possession by passing the ball back to a teammate in her own half, allowing time for attacking players to move ahead of the ball. It's important to teach your team to maintain possession at a kickoff and not just to kick the ball away to the other team.

The team that doesn't take the initial kickoff starts the second half with a kickoff. A kickoff is also taken to restart the game after a goal is scored, with the team that concedes the goal taking the kickoff. Soccer is a fast-flowing game and is continuous until the ball leaves the playing field, a goal is scored, or a foul is committed.

Scoring a Goal

To score a goal, one team must get the entire ball completely across the opponent's goal line between the goal posts and underneath the crossbar. You

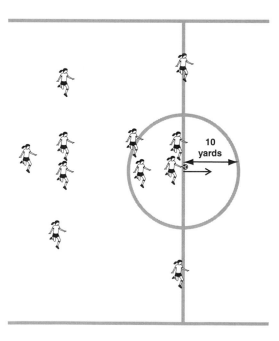

Positions when taking a kickoff.

10 yards

The ball is in play (1).

The ball is in play (2).

The ball is in play (3).

The ball is out of play (4).

must educate the players and parents that the ball doesn't have to hit the net for a goal to be scored. If a defender is able to stop the ball before it completely crosses over the goal line, it's not a goal.

Out of Play

When the ball leaves the playing area, the game temporarily stops. Because the lines are part of the playing area, the entire ball must completely cross the goal line or the sideline to be out of play. This can be on the ground or in the air.

When a team causes the ball to cross over the sideline, a *throw-in* is taken by the opposing team to bring the ball back into play. When the ball crosses over the goal line (but not between the goal posts), a *corner kick* is taken if the ball was last touched by the defending team, and a *goal kick* is taken if the attacking team was the last to touch it. If the ball crosses over the

Coaching Advice

"With 5- and 6-year-olds who are still learning to control and pass, the ball will leave the playing area often. As your goal is to help make the game flow and to maximize players' time with the ball, let them play beyond the boundaries if need be. Keep a ball in your hands so you can roll it into play and control where the game is being played."

Coaching Advice

"If beginners and young players are unable to control the ball when it arrives midair, they'll have considerable difficulty dealing with throw-ins. In order for the ball to be controlled and the game to continue quickly, allow the girls to pass the ball in to play."

Taking a throw-in. Hold the ball firmly with two hands and keep both feet on the ground (1).

Throw the ball from behind the head with both hands (2).

Follow through with the upper body (3).

goal line between the goal posts and underneath the crossbar, a goal is scored, and a kickoff results.

Throw-In

A throw-in is taken from the point where the ball crossed over the sideline. It can be taken by any player on the team. Every girl must be able to make a throw-in and must think of it as a way of getting the ball back in play as quickly as possible while keeping possession. There is no need to spend considerable time on throw-ins, but to avoid possible foul throws and loss of possession, each girl must learn the proper technique. This can be done as part of a warm-up or when teaching ball control.

How to Take a Throw-In

1. Stand behind the line
2. Keep both feet on the ground
3. Position two hands behind the ball, with thumbs just apart
4. Hold the ball with two hands throughout the throw-in
5. Take ball behind the head
6. Arch the back
7. Throw the ball from behind the head with both hands and snap the body forward
8. Aim the throw so the ball arrives at the receiving player quickly
9. Throw the ball down to teammate's feet so that she can pass the ball on her first touch

Coaching Advice

"It's extremely rare to find girls under the age of 13 who are able to take accurate corner kicks, and it's even rarer to find girls who are then able to head or volley the ball into the goal. In order to maintain possession and create scoring opportunities from corner kicks with young girls, teach and develop the *short corner*. Instead of the kicker booting the ball hopelessly toward goal with no purpose, she quickly plays a short pass of 2 or 3 yards to a second girl, who then dribbles toward goal. The girl who takes the corner kick sprints around her teammate, providing an option for the return pass. When pressured, the player with the ball can either beat the defender on the dribble or pass the ball back out to the first girl. With the ball now much closer to the goal, a shot can be taken or an accurate pass can be played to an open player."

Goal Kick

If the ball crosses over the goal line after being last played or touched by the attacking team, a goal kick is taken to bring the ball back into play. The ball is placed on the ground anywhere inside the 6-yard area and isn't in play until it's traveled beyond the penalty area. Any player on the defending team may take the goal kick and cannot touch the ball a second time until it's been touched by another player. When a goal kick is being taken, all players from the opposing team must be outside the penalty area. A goal cannot be scored directly from a goal kick.

Corner Kick

If the ball crosses over the goal line after being last played or touched by the defending team, a corner kick is taken to bring the ball back into play. The corners of the field are marked with a 1-yard arc. The ball is placed inside the corner area closest to where it went out of bounds. Any player on the attacking team may take the corner kick and cannot touch the ball a second time until it's been touched by another player. When a corner kick is taken, the defending team must be at least 10 yards away from the corner arc. The ball is not considered to be in play until it's left this arc. A goal can be scored directly from a corner kick.

Free Kick

When the rules of the game are broken, a *free kick* is awarded to the opposing team. A free kick can be either direct or indi-

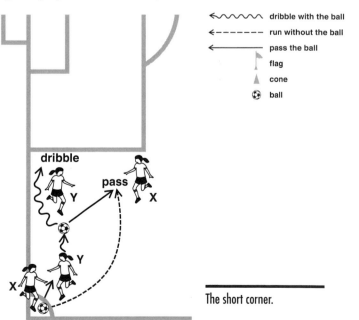

dribble with the ball
run without the ball
pass the ball
flag
cone
ball

The short corner.

rect. The difference between the two is simple but needs explaining to both parents and players to avoid confusion. A goal can be scored from a direct free kick but not from an indirect free kick. The referee indicates that an indirect free kick has been awarded by blowing the whistle and raising an arm straight up in the air. (See the illustration of referee signals on page 184.)

Direct Free Kick. A *direct free kick* is awarded if a serious foul is committed, such as kicking, tripping, hitting, pushing, pulling, spitting, or striking at an opponent. In addition, if the hands and arms are used to play the ball or if the goalkeeper handles the ball outside of her penalty area, a direct free kick is awarded. The kick must be taken where the incident occurred. The opposition must be 10 yards away from the ball when the kick is taken. If the incident or foul occurs inside the penalty area, a penalty kick is awarded.

Penalty Kick. A *penalty kick* is taken from the penalty spot, 12 yards from the goal. The goalkeeper must stand on her goal line and is not allowed to move forward until the kick is taken. All other players must be outside the penalty area and at least 10 yards behind the ball. With younger girls playing on smaller fields using smaller goals, many leagues and associations reduce the distance of the penalty kick from 12 to 8 yards.

Indirect Free Kick. An *indirect free kick* must be touched by at least two players before a goal can be scored. It's awarded for less serious offenses, such as deliberate obstruction, a high foot, offside, time wasting, and unsportsmanlike behavior. It's also awarded for many goalkeeper offenses, including holding the ball in the hands for longer than 6 seconds and using the hands to play the ball from a teammate's back pass.

The kick must be taken where the incident occurred. The opposition must be at least 10 yards away from the ball when an indirect free kick is taken. If an indirect free kick is awarded inside the penalty area and less than 10 yards from the goal, the opposition must be positioned on the goal line.

The Offside Rule

The offside rule is used to prevent players from just waiting in front of the opponent's goal for the ball to come to them. It's a rule that isn't used with younger players on small fields. When the rule is introduced into the game, it can lead to confusion among players and parents if not properly understood by the coach. US Youth Soccer recommends introducing the offside rule when players reach 9 or 10 years of age. In practice, keep things simple and only call players offside if they're clearly goal hanging.

Confusion often arises with the offside rule because a player can be in an offside position without being offside. The following examples will help explain and demonstrate the offside rule.

Being in an Offside Position. An attacking player is in an offside position if she is in her opponent's half of the field and there are fewer than two defensive players between her and the goal. (The goalkeeper is often one of these

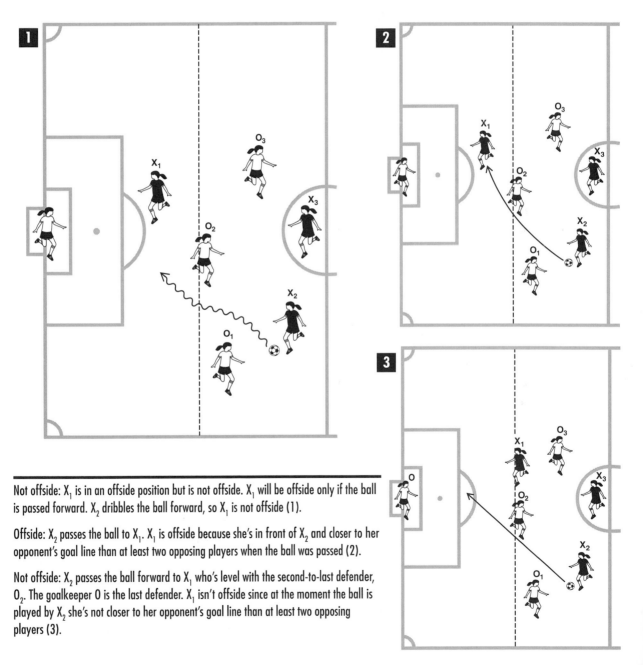

Not offside: X_1 is in an offside position but is not offside. X_1 will be offside only if the ball is passed forward. X_2 dribbles the ball forward, so X_1 is not offside (1).

Offside: X_2 passes the ball to X_1. X_1 is offside because she's in front of X_2 and closer to her opponent's goal line than at least two opposing players when the ball was passed (2).

Not offside: X_2 passes the ball forward to X_1 who's level with the second-to-last defender, O_2. The goalkeeper O is the last defender. X_1 isn't offside since at the moment the ball is played by X_2 she's not closer to her opponent's goal line than at least two opposing players (3).

players.) If the second defensive player is level with the attacker, then she is not considered to be in an offside position.

Being Offside. A player becomes offside if she's in an offside position at the moment her team passes the ball forward and she becomes involved in the play. If the ball is dribbled forward, passed backward, or played by the opposition, she's not offside. If she's in an onside position at the moment the ball is passed forward, she's also not offside.

Deciding if a girl is offside can be difficult and controversial for professional officials to call, so with volunteers and youth referees officiating, it's important to respect their decision at all times and to help your players understand how they can avoid being called offside if in the same situation.

Providing your team with an understanding of the offside rule can help tactically, as your forwards will know how far up the field they're able to stretch the opposition, and the defenders will know when to move up the field, leaving opponents in offside positions.

CHAPTER 6

Coaching the Season

In order to make each soccer experience as enjoyable and rewarding as possible and to maximize player development, you need to have a long-term outlook for each season. For the season to run smoothly, you need to be organized and have a plan for every practice, game, and meeting. Players and parents need to know what to do if it rains, what times practices will be, where to get uniforms, and a whole bunch more. It can be a huge undertaking for one person to do everything, so from the very start get some help from the other parents and delegate certain responsibilities. At the very least, ask somebody to be the assistant coach and somebody to be the team manager.

Tryouts

With girls under the age of 8, the club or league often assigns players to a certain coach in order to keep teams with the same number of players. As the girls get older and the games become more competitive, a tryout is usually held to decide who plays on what team.

At some stage you'll more than likely have to organize and run a tryout to select girls for your team. This is often the first look you'll get at your new players and potential team. During a tryout you must observe and evaluate each player's ability and select those girls who are the best combination for the team. You must plan the tryout so that you can assess all aspects of the game from their technical ability to their physical ability.

Meet the Parents

Before a soccer ball has been kicked, you need to meet with the parents to discuss many important issues, such as team rules, playing time, punctuality, sportsmanship, attendance at practice, finances, player development, and your goals, philosophy, and expectations.

This meeting should cover the following areas:

1. Introductions
2. Philosophy of player development
3. Long- and short-term goals
4. Team rules
5. Playing time, punctuality, and attendance
6. Request for some help from parents
7. Collection of vital player and parent contact information
8. Rain plan
9. Season practices: where, when, how often, and how long

Philosophy

The parents need to understand the difference between a philosophy of player development and one of short-term team success. You must explain to them and remind them frequently over the course of the season that it's easy to play a "kick and run" style of soccer with children in order to win games. This style, however, fails to develop players technically to play the game at a higher level when they're older. Once parents can see improvement in their daughter's playing ability and have learned to base success on individual and team performance rather than wins and losses, they'll become your most loyal supporters. If you look for short-term success and place emphasis on the results of the games, the parents will judge you and the team on results and will likely be supportive only when the team is winning.

Explain to the parents that a philosophy of player development doesn't mean that winning isn't important, nor does it teach the girls that to win isn't important. Obviously the objective of soccer is to beat the other team by scoring more goals. It just means that overall player development is more of a priority than the result of a single game. As the team gets older and the girls reach high school, a greater emphasis can be placed on results.

Long-Term Goals

Outline the long-term goals for the team over the next few years based on the age and ability of the players. Highlight the importance of prioritizing when different techniques and tactics are introduced, so that the girls are given the opportunity to master the basics of the game before advancing to more complex skills. Explaining to the parents of 8-year-olds why the majority of the practices will be geared toward dribbling, ball control, and passing and less on shooting and positioning will prevent parents from questioning what you're doing. Discuss the differences between being a recreational team, where players are allowed to play multiple sports, or a more competitive team, where soccer takes priority over all other sports. Finally, outline your short-term goals for the season, such as creating a fun learning environment, what techniques you want to teach, and any future events or tournaments that you plan on attending.

Team Rules

Your team rules should set out how both the parents and players should act at practices and during games, what the mandatory requirements are for attendance at practices and games, and the importance of punctuality. Initially, get the parents to agree on team rules, but once the girls are around age 11, it's good to get them involved in the process of establishing their own rules. When setting up your team rules, it's beneficial to let the parents or players make suggestions and to guide them into agreeing on rules, rather than just telling them what the rules are. If the parents or players come up with the rules, they're more likely to respect and follow those rules. While agreeing on the rules doesn't mean that they'll always be followed, it does mean that everybody knows what they are and what is expected.

The parents can be very enthusiastic during games and sometimes want to do more than just cheer on the team. They need to be told strongly that although it's important for them to be supportive of their daughter during the games, at no time should they try to give instruction or criticize. Explain to the parents that players become confused if they're taught to do something one way but are told by their parents to do it another way, and their overall development can be restricted. To maintain player confidence and overall self-esteem, it's vital that parents understand the effect that negative comments and criticism can have on young girls and also the role that confidence plays in soccer performance.

You must have a rule regarding sportsmanship so that the parents understand that at no time is it OK to yell or scream at the officials or opposition. They must treat the referee and other team with respect and set the example for all the players. The parents' behavior strongly influences the behavior of their daughter.

Playing Time, Practice Attendance, and Punctuality

The girls will be driven to practice by their parents, so the parents need to be aware of the importance of attendance and punctuality. While you need to have flexibility and be understanding of parental and sibling conflicts, the parents also need to know that it's not all right to miss or arrive late to practices. By making a commitment to the team, they have committed to come and be at the practices and games. Should parents be unable to get their daughter to practice on time suggest making arrangements with other parents to carpool. A great way of controlling and dealing with the issue of attendance and punctuality is to directly relate it to playing time. A certain amount of playing time may be guaranteed only if a player is on time and in attendance at practice. At this first meeting announce your general philosophy on playing time, such as whether or not every player will be guaranteed equal time or at least half a game, and if playing time is in any way connected to attendance at practice and punctuality.

Getting Help

Getting other parents to help you out, delegating different jobs, and selecting the right person to be the assistant coach or team manager will go a long way to ensuring that your role as coach is much easier and that you spend less time doing paperwork and more time teaching and coaching. Begin by finding out what each parent is able to do to help the team.

Select two or three parents to be in charge of fundraising. They'll be responsible for coming up with ideas and putting into place schemes to raise money for tournaments, uniforms, and camps.

Select a team manager to be responsible for registering players, completing forms, ordering uniforms, sending out information via phone chains or e-mail, and arranging events. Ask the manager to set up a calendar for the season indicating such things as team dinners, pasta nights, and the schedule for half-time snacks and setting up the goal nets. Having a good and reliable team manger will make your job much easier, so look to select somebody who's organized and has the time to help out.

Select an assistant coach to help you with practices and games. This should be somebody who understands your philosophy of coaching and player development, team rules, and sportsmanship. The assistant coach is responsible for helping at the practices and games and also for running the practices if you're unavailable. During the games you may want to have the assistant coach be in charge of playing time, substitutions, and preparing the goalkeeper for the game. The more responsibility you give to the assistant coach, the more involved he or she will feel and the more motivated to help.

Collect Vital Information

In order for information to be distributed quickly and for parents to be contacted in case of an emergency, you must collect contact information for both parents. Gather first and last names, addresses, phone numbers at home and work, cell phone numbers, and e-mail addresses. You must also find out if any of the girls have any medical conditions such as asthma, diabetes, or allergies.

Rain Plan

If the weather is severe or the fields are unplayable, you'll need to cancel practice, so a rain plan is needed. As the girls often have to play games in the rain, you should get them used to practicing in the rain and only cancel practice if the weather is severe.

If you're going to cancel a practice, make this decision at least 2 hours beforehand, to give time for the parents to get the message. The easiest way to let everybody know a practice or game is cancelled is with e-mail and a phone chain. The e-mail list should contain both work and home addresses so parents will receive the message whether they're at home or work. A standard e-mail can be set up that can be sent out to all families at the click of a button. If severe weather such as thunder and lightning arrives while you're at the field, a phone chain is the only way to get the message out to everybody. The phone chain should include both home and work numbers and also cell phone numbers as some people may already be on their way to practice.

Phone Chains

A phone chain is a simple and effective way to get a message by telephone to a group of people. You make an initial phone call to the team manager, who then calls two families. These two families call the next two families in the chain, who in turn call the next two. It's important that every contact number provided is called until a parent or player is spoken to. If there's no answer, a message should be left. If the home, work, and cell numbers have all been called but only messages left, the person calling must also call the next two players in the chain.

Travel Plans

The parents need to be given directions to the fields and know what time they need to be there for each game. Announce this at the first meeting of the season. Players aged 5–9 should meet 30 minutes before kickoff. Players aged 10–13 should meet 45 minutes before, and older players up to an hour before kickoff.

If you receive your game schedule before the start of the season, find the location of the

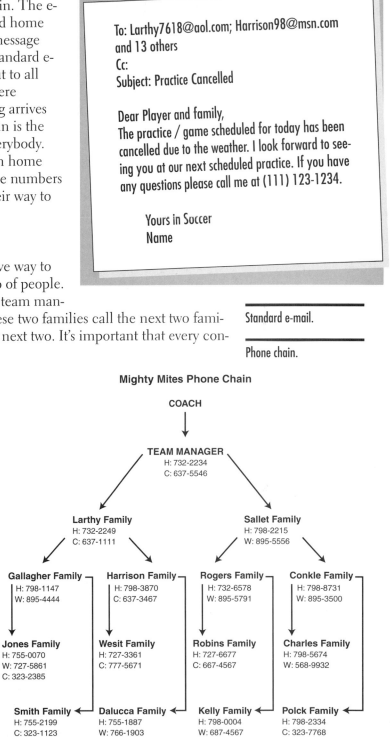

To: Larthy7618@aol.com; Harrison98@msn.com and 13 others
Cc:
Subject: Practice Cancelled

Dear Player and family,
The practice / game scheduled for today has been cancelled due to the weather. I look forward to seeing you at our next scheduled practice. If you have any questions please call me at (111) 123-1234.

Yours in Soccer
Name

Standard e-mail.

Phone chain.

Mighty Mites Phone Chain

COACH

TEAM MANAGER
H: 732-2234
C: 637-5546

Larthy Family
H: 732-2249
C: 637-1111

Sallet Family
H: 798-2215
W: 895-5556

Gallagher Family
H: 798-1147
W: 895-4444

Harrison Family
H: 798-3870
C: 637-3467

Rogers Family
H: 732-6578
W: 895-5791

Conkle Family
H: 798-8731
W: 895-3500

Jones Family
H: 755-0070
W: 727-5861
C: 323-2385

Wesit Family
H: 727-3361
C: 777-5671

Robins Family
H: 727-6677
C: 667-4567

Charles Family
H: 798-5674
W: 568-9932

Smith Family
H: 755-2199
C: 323-1123

Dalucca Family
H: 755-1887
W: 766-1903

Kelly Family
H: 798-0004
W: 687-4567

Polck Family
H: 798-2334
C: 323-7768

away games and get driving directions from your hometown. Save these in a file and give them out at the last practice before the game. In addition, send out an e-mail with the directions at the end of the week. If you have a team website, you can post all the directions for the season online for the parents to access and download at any time. With each set of directions it's useful to give an estimated driving time so that each driver allows plenty of time to get to the field.

Practice Schedule

Before you're able to plan what you want to teach and how many practices you want to set aside to learn and master each technique, you must decide for the season how often and how long you'll practice. Deciding whether you'll practice once, twice, or three times a week will depend on the age of your team, the commitment level, and your availability.

Decide on and announce the time and location for practices. If you're going to be practicing at different locations on different days, the parents may need directions for each field or park. Whenever you need to change practice time or location, always try to give notice ahead of time so that the parents can make suitable arrangements.

Questions and Answers

Q. The assistant coach who was assigned to help me out with the team has had some experience coaching soccer, but unfortunately her ideas and methods are very traditional. She believes in running the girls for 15 minutes at the start of every practice and performing drills one at a time in lines. What should I do?

A. As the head coach, you need to take the time to listen to her ideas. Her help with the team is important, so you must try to keep her motivated and involved. Explain to her your beliefs and the reasons why you'd like her to do things a certain way, even though she's more comfortable doing them another way. She needs to be educated about soccer development and the importance of providing every player with as many touches of the ball as possible. Give her very specific instructions about her role as the assistant coach and how you would like her to organize the practices when you're not there.

Q. What's the best way to communicate information to the parents and players during the season?

A. You should use a variety of different methods to communicate, such as e-mail, handouts, meetings, and phone chains. The simplest way is probably to e-mail everybody with information, but you'll need to make other arrangements for those without e-mail service. In addition, always have a team meeting at the start of every season, midway through the season, and at the end of season to communicate and reinforce your coaching philosophy, pass on any future information, and answer any questions. Even better still, have a brief meeting with the parents after each game to communicate information.

At the end of practice distribute a handout with information and directions for the upcoming game. In case parents lose this sheet and also to remind everybody, e-mail the information again the day before the game. Another way to quickly communicate information such as rain cancellations, directions, and changes in practice times is to set up a team website that the parents can access at any time from work or home. So, you'll find yourself communicating to parents throughout the season through a variety of methods.

Q. Who sets up my practice and game schedule?

A. Most clubs and leagues will set up the schedule of games and fields to be used. Call the opposing coach a few days before the game to double-check the location and time and to make sure nothing has changed. If field space is restricted in your neighborhood, the club or league may also be responsible for scheduling when and where you can practice. If not, then locate a school field or town park that's convenient and check to see if a club permit is needed before using it.

CHAPTER 7

Essential Techniques

Dribbling Exercises and Games

Use the following exercises and games (described in detail in Chapters 12, 13, and 15) to improve dribbling skills:

Soccer is a game involving four components: tactical, physical, psychological, and technical. By far the most important to develop is the technical component, involving seven fundamental soccer techniques. Without these techniques, development of the other components becomes useless. There's no point in developing mentally tough girls who can run faster and longer than others if they're unable to control or pass the ball accurately and therefore give the ball away. Teaching and improving the technical ability of your girls should therefore be your first priority, with emphasis on the other components coming once the basic techniques have been learned. The seven basic techniques that need to be mastered are dribbling, passing, ball control, shooting and finishing, heading, defending, and goalkeeping. This chapter will prepare you to teach and coach each technique.

Dribbling

Dribbling is the ability of a player to move comfortably and confidently with the ball, using her feet. It's possibly the most important basic technique in soccer. Girls must learn to move the ball with the inside, outside, instep, and sole of each foot and do so with their heads up to assess what's happening around them in the game. They must be able to move upfield with the ball, quickly changing direction and beating defenders with dribbling moves and fakes, and when required they must be able to protect and shield the ball. Dribbling situations can be put into one of three categorizes, each requiring a different technique: speed dribbling, dribbling to change direction, and dribbling to beat defenders.

The best way to teach dribbling is through fun games that allow the girls to have hundreds of touches of the ball with different parts of their feet. The more touches each girl has, the better she becomes, so avoid dribbling lines at all costs.

Remember: No Lines, No Laps, and No Lectures (see pages 109–10).

There are many fun games to practice dribbling in Chapter 12 of this book. Many of the games involve catchers and are designed to keep players moving around, changing direction with their heads up without losing control of the ball or being caught by the catchers.

Speed Dribbling

Speed dribbling is used when a girl is in open space and wants to move up-field with the ball as fast as possible while maintaining possession. Have the girls move around with the ball in a small area using just their feet. On your command they must quickly move to a new area 30–40 yards away, dribbling from one area to the other as fast as possible while keeping control of the ball.

How to Teach Speed Dribbling.

- Move the ball forward using a long running stride
- Push the ball forward without breaking stride
- When pushing the ball forward, point the toe down and the foot slightly inward so that contact with the ball is made between the toe and the laces
- Run as fast as possible, keeping the ball at a distance that requires a minimal number of touches to move it forward
- Always keep this distance close enough so that control of the ball isn't lost

Dribbling to Change Direction

Dribbling to change direction is used when a girl is in a tight area and must move into open space to maintain possession. If several defenders approach a girl from her left, she may change direction and go to the right. A girl may change direction quickly to put a defender off balance so as to create space for a pass or a shot. There are many moves that can be used while dribbling to change direction. In each case the girl must maintain her balance and keep control of the ball at all times.

Dribble the ball, keeping the head up, and push the ball forward into open space without breaking stride (left).

Make contact with the ball between the toe and the laces (right).

Dribbling to Beat Defenders

Dribbling to beat defenders is used to move the ball into the space behind an opposing player. Girls must utilize dribbling moves and fakes to get defenders off balance and then change direction and speed to move past them. Once again possession of the ball must be maintained once the defender has been beaten.

To set up this dribbling environment, play a game by creating a large area in which the girls can move around with the ball. Try to catch every player by touching their ball with the sole of your foot. The girls, however, can freeze you for 2 seconds by performing a dribbling move. This gives them enough time to escape and prevents them from being caught. If caught, the girls must leave the area and perform a forfeit before reentry. This is usually a set number of juggles or a set number of repetitions of the dribbling move that's being learned. After you've played the game a few times, select two girls to be the new catchers.

How to Teach Dribbling to Change Direction and Beat Defenders.

- Keep the ball within playing distance at all times but not right underneath the feet
- Don't keep the ball too close to the body when dribbling
- Move around with the head up, assessing the field for open space and open players
- Accelerate with the ball into open space
- Change speed and direction when dribbling past defenders
- Use moves when dribbling to fake out defenders and get them off balance

Dribbling Moves

Coaching Advice

"When teaching dribbling moves, always have the girls practice the moves with both feet."

There are many different dribbling moves ranging from the simple to the complex, with new moves being devised all the time. Often moves are named after the players who mastered them. The following are essential dribbling moves that can be taught to and performed by beginners but that take many hours of practice and repetition before being executed successfully in games. The essential moves are the drag back, roll flick, Cryuff turn, outside cut, stop turn, L-shape move, scissors, and squeeze push.

Common Problems and Corrections

Problem: The girls dribble with the inside of the feet only or use just one foot. **Correction:** Different parts of both feet need to be used, so teach and encourage the girls to move the ball around with all parts of their feet. They need to be able to move the ball quickly from one foot to the other.

Stages of the drag back.
Dribble forward, keeping the ball under control (1).

Place the sole of the foot on the ball (2).

Bend at the knees and drag the ball back in the opposite direction (3).

Push the ball away with the outside of the same foot (4).

How to Teach the Drag Back. The drag back is also called the pull back or roll back and is used often at all levels in soccer to change and move in an opposite direction.

- If the defender is on the left side, use the right foot, and vice versa
- While dribbling, place the sole of the foot on the top of the ball
- With the sole of the foot drag the ball backward 180°
- Turn in the same direction as the foot used to drag the ball (if using the right foot, turn to the right, opening up the body)
- After turning, push the ball away with the outside of the same foot (if turning to the right, use the right foot)
- Accelerate away in the new direction
- Keep the ball in view and within playing distance at all times during the move

How to Teach the Roll Flick. The roll flick is similar to the drag back except the ball moves through 90°. It's often used when a player is pressured and has little space.

- While dribbling, place the sole of one foot on the top of the ball; if the defender is on the right side, use the left foot, and vice versa
- With the sole of the foot, drag the ball backward until the ball is behind the nonkicking foot
- While the ball is still rolling, flick it quickly with the inside of the same foot so that the ball moves at a 90° angle
- Accelerate away in the new direction
- Push the ball away with the outside of the nonkicking foot

How to Teach the Cryuff Turn. The Cryuff turn is named after the Dutch maestro Johan Cryuff, who made this his signature move. In this turn the player fakes striking the ball with the instep of the foot and then quickly changes direction.

- While dribbling, place the nonkicking foot alongside the ball

Stages of the Cryuff turn. Position the upper body as if about to strike the ball (1).

Use the inside of the kicking foot to make contact with the front of the ball (2).

Bend the knees and pull the ball backward with the inside of the foot (3).

Turn and take the ball away with the outside of the opposite foot (4).

- Position the upper body as if about to strike the ball with the laces
- Instead of striking the ball, move the kicking foot in front of it and turn the ankle 90° inward so that the inside of the foot is in contact with the front of the ball
- Bend the knees to lower the center of gravity
- Using the inside of the kicking foot, pull the ball backward in the opposite direction
- Turn and pivot and take the ball away with the outside of your opposite foot (the nonkicking foot)
- Accelerate away in the new direction

How to Teach the Outside Cut. This is a very common move with girls and involves turning 180° with the outside of the foot.

- While dribbling and being pressured from the left, move the ball away from this defender to the outside of the right foot
- Shield the ball with the upper body
- Move the right foot ahead of the ball and turn the ankle so that the outside of the foot makes contact with the ball

Stages of the outside cut. Dribble with the toe pointed down and the foot turned inward (1).

Move the outside of the foot ahead of the ball and turn the ankle outward (2).

Cut the ball with the outside of the foot and turn quickly (3).

Accelerate away in the opposite direction (4).

- Cut (flick) the ball with the outside of the right foot so that the ball moves backward in the opposite direction
- With the defender still moving forward, bend the knees to lower the center of gravity and pivot off the left leg to turn 180° with the ball
- Accelerate away in the new direction

How to Teach the Stop Turn. This is a move used to turn 180° when running with the ball at faster speeds.

- While running with the ball at speed and being pressured from the left, use the foot farthest away from the defender (in this case the right foot) to stop the ball dead with the sole of the foot
- Jump forward, moving the right foot and upper body sideways beyond the ball
- Bend the right knee
- Move the left leg over the ball
- With the outside of the left foot, take the ball in the opposite direction
- Accelerate away in the new direction

Stages of the stop turn.
Place the foot on top of the ball (1).

Use the sole of the foot to suddenly stop the ball (2).

Quickly shift the body beyond the ball (3).

Use the outside of the opposite foot to push the ball away (4).

How to Teach the L-Shape Move. This move, used to dribble past a defender, involves the ball moving in an L-shaped manner.

- While dribbling, shift the body and fake passing the ball to the right with the inside of the right foot (the hips and body open up—swiveling to the right—as if you were going to pass to the right with the inside of the right foot)
- Instead, play the ball with the inside of the right foot back across the body
- Quickly shift body weight and play the ball past the defender with the inside of the left foot
- Accelerate into the space behind the defender

How to Teach the Scissors. In this move the player fakes taking the ball with the outside of one foot and then accelerates into the space behind the defender on the opposite side. This is a move that all girls need to master with both feet.

Stages of the scissors.
Position the ball to the outside of the body (1).

Quickly step over the ball with the right leg (2).

Shift the upper body across the ball with the knees bent (3).

Push the ball away at 45° with the outside of the left foot (4).

- While dribbling, position the ball outside the right foot
- Fake to go to the right by shifting the upper body right
- Move the right leg and upper body over the ball
- With the defender off balance, immediately take the ball with the outside of the left foot at 45° into the space on the left
- Accelerate into the space behind the defender

How to Teach the Squeeze Push. This move is similar to the scissors, except quick movement of the ball is now involved in the fake. It's good for practicing using different parts of the foot.

- Dribble with the ball out in front and slightly to the right of the body
- Position the ball next to the inside of the right foot, with the knees slightly bent
- Roll the right foot over the ball so that it moves across the body from right to left, shifting the defender to the left
- With the knees bent, squeeze and push the ball with the outside of the right foot back away to the right of the defender
- Accelerate into the space

Stages of the squeeze push. Position the ball on the inside of the right foot with the knees slightly bent (1).

Keep the foot in contact with the ball as it moves across the body (2).

Roll the ball from the inside to the outside of the foot (3).

Bend the knees, squeezing the ball away with the outside of the foot (4).

Common Problems and Corrections

Problem: The defender is not faked by the scissors move. **Correction:** The girl is only stepping over the ball with her leg. She has to shift both her leg and upper body across the ball.

Problem: When the girl performs a move to go past a defender, the ball runs into the defender. **Correction:** She's performing the move too close to the defender and needs to give herself more space. This distance depends on ability, but for beginners 3–5 yards from the defender is a good distance.

Problem: After the girl has performed the move, she loses control of the ball. **Correction:** The ball is being kicked too far past the defender, so encourage the girl to just push the ball into the space instead of kicking it.

Passing

When the ball is kicked from one player to another, it's called a *pass*. The ability to pass the ball over short and long distances is the foundation of good team play. There are various types of pass, each requiring a different technique. The two basic techniques to pass over short distances are the inside foot pass and the outside foot pass, whereas the more advanced techniques to pass over longer distances include the driven pass, the lofted pass, the curved pass, and the chipped pass. It's important that girls master each passing technique and do so with each foot.

Inside Foot Pass

When passing the ball over short distances, the most accurate and easiest technique to use is the inside foot pass. This fundamental technique can and must be taught to girls from the age of 4 or 5.

How to Teach Passing with the Inside of the Foot.

- Place the nonkicking foot next to the ball, with the toe pointing in the direction of the target
- Aim the inside of the kicking foot at the target
- Make the inside of the kicking foot firm by locking the ankle
- Turn the toe of the kicking foot slightly upward
- Focus the eyes on the ball
- With the inside of the foot, strike through the center of the ball
- Follow through in the direction that you want the ball to travel

Coaching Advice

"In order to help 4- to 7-year-olds keep their ankles firm when passing the ball, go around and lock their ankles into the correct position with an imaginary magical key."

Passing Exercises and Games

Use the following exercises and games (described in detail in Chapters 12 and 15) to improve passing skills:

- Monsters, Inc. II **13**
- Stuck in the Mud **14**
- Smelly Egg **15**
- Dog Pound **16**
- Soccer Mall **17**
- Tunnel Run **18**
- Soccer Tennis **19**
- Numbered Passing **20**
- Keep-Away **21**
- Long Passing Gates **22**
- Four-on-Two Competition **23**
- Control Gates **36**
- Three-on-One World Cup **38**
- Four-on-One World Cup **71**
- Four-on-Two Intercept **72**

The inside foot pass. The ankle is firm, with the toe pointing slightly upward. The inside of the foot is aimed at the target and makes contact with the center of the ball. The nonkicking foot is next to the ball with the toe pointing in the direction of the target (left).

After the pass, the inside of the foot remains facing the direction of the pass and follows through toward the target. Notice how the eyes focus on the ball (right).

Common Problems and Corrections

Problem: The pass is too soft. **Correction:** The ball hasn't been played with enough power, so have the girl approach the ball with a slight run up. The momentum of her moving will be transferred into the ball. Have her follow through the ball instead of stopping once contact with the ball has been made.

Problem: The ball goes in the air. **Correction:** The girl is getting underneath the ball on contact, so have her focus on a mark in the center of the ball and strike the ball at this point. Make sure the nonkicking foot is alongside the ball, for the ball will also go in the air if the foot is behind.

Problem: The pass isn't on target. **Correction:** The girl's feet are out of position. Make sure the toe of her nonkicking foot and the inside of her kicking foot are both aimed at the target. Check that her follow-through is also in the direction of the target.

Outside Foot Pass

The outside foot pass is commonly used by players while running with the ball, because the pass can be made without breaking stride. It's more difficult to read, as it's disguised within the running stride, which often captures the opposition by surprise.

How to Teach Passing with the Outside of the Foot.

- Position the ball as if dribbling with the outside of the foot
- Position the nonkicking foot behind and to the side of the ball
- Position the kicking foot to the inside of the ball so that contact can be made with the outside of the foot
- Swing back the kicking leg from the knee and rotate the ankle slightly inward so that the outside of the foot is aimed at the ball

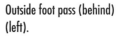

Outside foot pass (behind) (left).

Outside foot pass (front). The ankle must be turned inward so the outside of the foot can make contact with the inside of the ball (right).

Common Problems and Corrections

Problem: The pass is too soft. **Correction:** The pass doesn't have enough power. Let the girl pass while running with the ball. Have her increase the backswing of her leg and follow through the ball in the direction of the target player.

Problem: The pass isn't on target. **Correction:** The girl's foot must be angled so that the outside is facing the direction of the target player. Her follow-through should also be in this direction.

- Strike the inside of the ball and follow through in the direction of the target

Driven Pass

There's a distance at which the ball can't be passed with sufficient speed using the inside or outside foot pass. This distance changes with age and ability and will vary from player to player. Players must learn to understand which technique is appropriate for each passing situation. In order to pass the ball over longer distances, a range of different techniques can be used. The driven pass is used to pass the ball on the ground quickly over distances longer than can be played with the inside of the foot.

How to Teach the Driven Pass.
- Approach the ball at a slight angle, with a two- or three-step run up
- Position the nonkicking foot level with the ball and a few inches to the side, with the toe pointing in the direction of the target
- Point the toe of the kicking foot down toward the ground

Common Problems and Corrections

Problem: The pass is too soft. **Correction:** To create more power, a longer leg swing is required. The girl must approach the ball slightly from the side. Once again, make sure her leg and body follow through the ball and don't stop once contact with the ball has been made.

Problem: The pass isn't on target. **Correction:** The girl's kicking leg and body must follow through in the direction of the target. If the kicking leg goes off slightly to the left, then the pass will be off to the left, away from the intended target.

For the driven pass, place the nonkicking foot alongside the ball and point the toe of the kicking foot down to help keep the ball on the ground.

- Strike the center of the ball with the laces
- Keep the head down and the eyes focused on the ball throughout
- Follow through in the direction of the target

Lofted Pass

The lofted pass is similar to the driven pass, except it's used to pass the ball in the air quickly over longer distances.

How to Teach the Lofted Pass.

- Approach the ball at a slight angle, with a two- or three-step run up
- Position the nonkicking foot slightly behind the ball and a few inches to the side, with the toe pointing in the direction of the target
- Point the toe of the kicking foot down toward the ground
- Lean back slightly and strike below the center of the ball with the laces
- Follow through in the direction of the target

When lofting a pass, position the nonkicking foot slightly behind the ball and strike the bottom half of the ball to help lift it off the ground.

Common Problems and Corrections

Problem: The ball won't go in the air. **Correction:** To lift the ball over a defender, the girl must strike underneath the ball. The nonkicking foot should be positioned slightly behind the ball, and the kicking foot comes off the ground during the follow-through.

Coaching Advice

"Girls develop less muscle mass than boys following puberty and generally find it more difficult to play longer passes. Time must therefore be spent mastering the technique of both the driven and lofted pass so girls become more proficient at playing these longer passes."

Ball Control

Players must be able to receive passes and have the ball under control with a minimal number of touches. They do this using various parts of the body, such as the feet, thighs, chest, or head, and must be able to do so in a manner that allows them to then pass, dribble, or shoot the ball. The *first touch* a girl has when receiving the pass is what determines how well the ball is controlled.

Learning to control the ball and developing a good first touch are key fundamentals for future soccer success because these skills allow players to have time to perform the other aspects of the game. Players are able to get their head up and make good decisions regarding space, possession, and attacking.

Mastering ball control and the first touch must begin at the earliest possible age and are best developed by allowing each girl to spend as much time as possible with the ball. Every part of the body except the hands and arms can be used to control the ball, and because the ball often arrives in the air or bouncing, each girl must be comfortable using her thighs, chest, head, and feet.

Juggling

Juggling is a term used to refer to keeping the ball under control in the air without using the hands and arms and is a vital tool in the development of every girl's ball control. Girls should use their feet and thighs to juggle the ball and with improvement should experiment using other body parts including the head, shoulders, chest, outside of the foot, and heel.

Becoming a master of the ball doesn't happen overnight. It takes many hours of practice and individual time with the ball. Juggling must be practiced every day and must be part of every practice at every age.

It's very unlikely that a group of 5-year-olds will be able to do more than two juggles, as they have very little eye-foot coordination and have no feel for the ball. So begin with catch juggles where each girl must drop the ball onto her thigh and then catch it. Every time the girls do a catch juggle they say a letter of their name and continue until they can spell their whole name. This can be achieved quite quickly, allowing them to move on to catch juggles using the foot. Players drop the ball toward the ground and then use the top of the foot to kick the ball back up into the air so they can catch it.

When teaching juggling with girls, it's important to make it fun and challenging for all. There will be some girls who can juggle well and others who can't, so it's vital to focus on individual improvement. Be careful that girls who are less proficient at juggling are not discouraged by challenges. If you challenge the group to see who can be the first to achieve 20 juggles, you'll be motivating only those girls who are close to achieving this goal. Those girls who can do only 5 juggles will feel discouraged and unmotivated,

Ball Control Exercises and Games

Use the following exercises and games (described in detail in Chapter 12) to develop players' skills at ball control:

- Soccer Mall **17**
- Soccer Tennis **19**
- Pumpkin Picking **34**
- First-Touch Races **35**
- Control Gates **36**
- Stop and Go **37**
- Three-on-One World Cup **38**
- Air Control **39**
- Control Squares **40**

Juggling Exercises and Games

Use the following exercises and games (described in detail in Chapter 12) to improve juggling skills:

- Catch Juggles **24**
- Name Juggling **25**
- Bounce Juggling **26**
- Catch Juggling II **27**
- Total Body Juggling **28**
- Feet-Only Juggling **29**
- Thigh-Only Juggling **30**
- Juggling to the Goal **31**
- Partner Juggling **32**
- Sequential Feet Juggling **33**

as the challenge set is unrealistic for them. Instead focus on individual improvement by challenging each girl to beat her personal best by 2 juggles, a goal that can be achieved by the entire group.

How to Teach Juggling.

- Juggle the ball low to the ground when using the feet; if the ball is above the waist, use the thighs

Juggling. The surface of contact (in this case the top of the foot) is moved and positioned directly underneath the ball (1).

Notice how the eyes are focused on the ball and how the body is relaxed (2).

The arms are used to maintain balance (3).

Players should learn to juggle the ball with as many different body surfaces as possible (4).

- Use the top of the foot, with the toe pointed up, to give the ball a slight backspin
- If the ball is spinning in to the body, point the toe down slightly
- After each juggle, return the kicking foot to the ground to maintain balance and to allow small movements of the body position
- Move the body so the foot or thigh is always able to make contact below the ball
- If the ball is going away from the body after the touch, get the foot further underneath the ball or point the toe more upward
- With more advanced juggling, if the ball is spinning sideways left to right, contact the ball on the outside, and vice versa

By improving her juggling, each girl will develop her ball control and first touch. As the ball can arrive either on the ground or in the air at various speeds and heights, each player must learn a wide variety of ways for ball control.

Ball Control on the Ground

A ball that arrives on the ground is the simplest to control and involves having a first touch with the inside or outside of the foot into an open space. A good first touch allows the girl to lift her head up and assess the field, making quick decisions. If more than one touch is needed to control the ball, the head must go down again, leaving less time to then pass, shoot, or dribble the ball.

How to Teach Ball Control on the Ground.

- Move body in line with the path of the receiving ball
- Be alert and on the balls of the feet—"Be on your toes"
- Select which foot to use and which part of the foot to use to control the ball
- Turn the foot so the inside or outside of the foot is facing the ball
- Bend the knee of the receiving leg
- At contact, cushion the ball by moving the foot slightly backward
- Redirect the ball into the best attacking space so the ball keeps moving
- In open space take the first touch to the side that allows the next touch to be a dribble, shot, or pass
- In pressured space take the first touch away from the defender
- Consider this first touch as a little pass to yourself

When controlling the ball on the ground, move the inside of the foot in line with the path of the ball. Notice how the body is over the ball (top).

Encourage players to cushion the ball on contact (bottom).

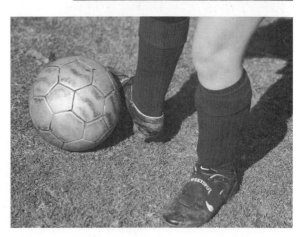

Common Problems and Corrections

Problem: The ball stops under the feet. **Correction:** Either the foot is positioned too far backward on contact with the ball and then stops, or the sole of the foot is used. In both situations another touch must be taken to get the ball out from under the feet before proceeding. Using the sole of the foot is poor technique. Emphasize that the girl is to make a small pass to herself.

Problem: The ball bounces off the foot. **Correction:** The foot is either stationary or moving forward when contact with the ball is made. There must be a soft backward motion of the foot so the ball is cushioned on contact.

Problem: The ball skips up in the air. **Correction:** The foot is getting underneath the ball. Contact must be made above the center of the ball to keep it on the ground. Encourage the girl to lean forward as she controls the ball.

Ball control in the air. No matter what height the ball is, it's important to move the controlling surface in line with the flight of the ball. Here the inside of the foot is used (1).

The body is positioned over the ball, and the inside of the foot is pressed into the upper half of the ball, keeping it on the ground (2).

Following the first touch, the player must immediately get her head up (3).

Ball Control in the Air

When the ball arrives in the air, a player must be able to control it with her feet, thighs, chest, and even sometimes her head. If a girl is able to control a high ball early with her chest, as opposed to allowing it to drop to her feet, she'll have more time on the ball to pass, shoot, or dribble. Encourage girls to use their thighs and feet to control balls below the waist, and the chest to control balls above the waist. Slight movement of the body forward or backward will allow the appropriate surface to be used.

How to Control Balls Low to the Ground Using the Feet.

- Get in line with the flight of the ball
- Focus the eyes on the ball

- Get the body over the ball as it drops
- As the ball hits the ground, use the inside or outside of the foot to press into the top side of the ball and push the ball away to the side
- Get the head up

How to Control Balls Higher in the Air Using the Feet.

- Get in line with the flight of the ball
- Using the arms to balance, lift the receiving foot to meet the ball at a point below the waist
- Decide which surface of the foot to use, depending on the spin of the ball
- As contact is made, cushion the ball by dropping the foot toward the ground
- Redirect the ball by pushing it into space
- Get the head up

Using the feet to control high balls. The foot is raised off the ground and positioned in line with the flight of the ball. Here the top of the foot is used to control the ball (1).

When the ball arrives, the foot is dropped toward the ground to cushion the ball (2).

How to Teach Thigh Control.

- Get in line with the flight of the ball
- Using the arms to balance, lift the receiving thigh to meet the ball
- On contact, cushion the ball by slightly moving the thigh down so that the ball drops to the ground, rather than bouncing up

Common Problems and Corrections

Problem: The ball keeps bouncing up off the thigh. **Correction:** On contact, the controlling body part must cushion the ball by moving away from it. It's common for youth players to favor one side of the body, such as using the right thigh to control a ball on the left. This often leads to the controlling surface moving toward the ball on contact as opposed to away from it. Using the appropriate body part will help maintain balance and cushion the ball.

Thigh control. With the body behind the ball, the receiving thigh is raised to meet it (1).

On contact, the thigh moves downward, cushioning the ball (2).

As the ball drops to the ground, the foot controls it into open space. Make sure to get the head up and look for space (3).

- As the ball hits the ground, press the inside or outside of the foot into the top side of the ball and push the ball away to the side
- Get the head up

How to Teach Chest Control.

- Get the chest in line with the flight of the ball
- Use the upper part of the chest directly below the shoulder blades

Chest control. Girls should keep their eyes open and move their whole body behind the ball (1).

The shoulders are pushed backward, the back is bent backward, and the chest is pushed out to control the ball (2).

- As the ball arrives, create a large surface area by pushing shoulders back and bending backward
- On contact, give at the knees and move the chest backward to cushion the ball; the chest should absorb the movement of the ball and let it drop to the ground

There's often a lack of confidence and nervousness in girls when controlling the ball with the chest. They must learn the correct technique and master it in order to improve and develop as players. Practicing chest control from a young age in a progressive manner will help build the confidence necessary to perform the technique successfully.

Progressive Chest Control for Girls.
- **Self-feed:** To build confidence, have the girls throw the ball to themselves in the air and have them cushion the ball using the correct technique.
- **Partner feed:** Have a partner gently throw the ball underarm toward each girl's chest.
- **Moving feed:** Have a partner gently throw the ball underarm in the space to the side of each girl so she must first move in line with the flight of the ball. Advance to feeding the ball harder and higher. Finally progress to controlling a throw-in and a lofted pass.

Shooting and Finishing

Scoring a goal is the ultimate objective in soccer, with goal scorers getting much of the attention and glory. *Shooting* and *finishing*, the techniques used to score goals, are what every young girl wants to excel at. It's often difficult in practice to re-create the game-like intensity in which shooting and finishing must occur, so they're some of the hardest aspects to master. (*Shooting* is a technique using the feet to strike at the goal—usually the instep, inside or outside. *Finishing* uses different parts of the body to score a goal. Scoring a goal with your head, knee, toe are techniques used in finishing.)

There are several techniques used to shoot and finish, with advanced players being able to chip the ball over goalkeepers, bend the ball around defenders, and score with spectacular volleys and overhead kicks. Girls must develop every technique and learn when to use each, a decision based on such factors as the distance from the goal, position of the goalkeeper, and the presence of pressuring defenders. All girls must learn to become proficient at shooting and finishing with both feet.

Girls must be able to finish and score goals using a variety of different techniques.

Instep shooting. Striking the ball with the instep is one of the hardest techniques for young girls to accomplish. Approach slightly from the side (1).

The toe of the nonkicking foot points in the direction of the shot (2).

The laces of the kicking foot strike through the center of the ball. Striking at the middle of the ball—not the top or bottom—makes the ball move with explosive power (3).

Instep Shooting

The first and most important technique that young girls must learn is shooting the ball from a distance with the instep.

How to Teach Instep Shooting.

- Approach the ball slightly from the side
- Position the nonkicking foot alongside the ball and a few inches to the side, with the toe pointing in the direction of the target
- Using the kicking foot, point the toe down, lock the ankle, and make contact with the instep (the laces)
- Strike through the center of the ball
- Lean forward and follow through the ball in the direction of the target
- Land on the foot that kicked the ball

Where to Strike the Ball. Striking and accelerating through the bottom of the ball causes it to move with a backward spin. This backward rotation slows the ball down considerably and causes it to hold up in the air, making it easier for goalkeepers to catch. Striking through the top half of the ball creates topspin, causing the ball to dip in the air and accelerate forward on bouncing. The ball moves much faster and is considerably more difficult for the goalkeeper to save.

Striking and accelerating through the middle of the ball creates no spin. This is a very difficult technique to master. Because the ball has no rotation, it moves with explosive power, literally accelerating toward the goal. It's very difficult for keepers to read the pace of the ball, so this is a very difficult shot to save. Teaching girls to technically strike the ball in this manner should be a goal of every youth coach.

Common Problems and Corrections

Problem: She's unable to get the ball on target. **Correction:** Usually the girl hasn't followed through in the direction in which she wants the ball to go, or her nonkicking foot isn't pointing at the target. If the girl follows through left of target, then the shot will veer off to the left. Also check to make sure the girl is striking the middle of the ball. If she scuffs the side of the ball, the shot will be off target.

Problem: She keeps shooting over the goal. **Correction:** Make sure the girl's nonkicking foot is correctly placed alongside the ball and not behind it. Have her strike through the center of the ball and not the bottom of the ball. Finally, have her lean forward and follow through, landing on her kicking foot.

Problem: She keeps shooting at the goalkeeper. **Correction:** Before the girl strikes the ball, have her lift her head or use her peripheral vision to assess the position of the goalkeeper. Her nonkicking foot must point into the space away from the keeper, and she also must follow through in this direction.

Problem: There's no power in the shot. **Correction:** The power comes from the momentum of the body and kicking leg being transferred into the ball, so make sure the girl follows through when striking. She must accelerate through the ball and not follow through slowly. If she's stopping or falling backward at contact, then little or no power will be generated into the shot.

Accuracy before Power. Whenever you're coaching youth players, emphasis must always be placed on accuracy before power, for you can't score if the shot isn't on target. Older male soccer players are often able to shoot and score by striking the ball with so much power that the goalkeeper is unable to react quickly enough to make the save. A female's leg strength doesn't develop to the same extent, however, so women are unable to generate the same degree of power as their male counterparts. It's vital, therefore, that girls strike the ball with a high degree of accuracy to score past the goalkeeper.

Finishing

Finishing often involves selecting an appropriate technique to shoot on goal. The technique used is dependent on the position of the defenders, the amount of time on the ball, and the position of the goalkeeper. To select the appropriate technique, girls must learn to lift their heads and assess the finishing situation in a split second. When striking with the instep, aim for the far post so that if the shot on goal is saved, the opportunity for a rebound will present itself.

Players will often find themselves in front of the goal with very little time, so *first-time finishing*—redirecting the ball with one touch to score a goal—must become automatic and instinctive. Girls can finish by flicking the ball past the goalkeeper with the inside and outside of the foot, the instep, and even the toe. Emphasis is on accuracy, redirecting the ball away from the goalkeeper. To avoid first-time finishes flying over the top of the goal, players must lean forward and follow through the ball.

An ability to finish with both feet is essential. If, for example, a girl is

Coaching Advice

"As with all aspects of soccer, players need to be given the maximum opportunity to practice both the technique of shooting and the art of finishing. Avoid lining up the girls and letting them shoot one at a time, for this doesn't provide them with maximum repetitions or realistic finishing situations. Create small-group games and situations where they have many chances to practice shooting and finishing."

in the 6-yard box and directly facing the goal as the ball is crossed from the right, it's nearly impossible for that player to score with the inside of the right foot. She must have practiced and be able to finish using her left foot.

Heading

Heading is the use of the forehead to play the ball when it's in the air. The head is used to control the ball, pass the ball, clear the ball, score goals, and win possession. It's a vital technique of the game but one that many girls find intimidating. Many young players fear that they might get hurt or hit in the face, so it's essential that they develop confidence at an early age. Girls must be taught the correct technique of heading so that they're able to play the ball safely and confidently with their head.

Note: Soccer is one of the world's oldest sports and is played by more people than any other sport. There's no evidence that the technique of heading a ball when playing soccer causes injury or an adverse effect on an individual's brain.

How to Teach Heading.

- Keep the eyes open throughout and focused on the ball
- Use the forehead to make contact with the ball
- Bend at the knees and the waist
- Use the arms and upper body to thrust the head and neck forward to meet the ball
- If heading to attack or pass, head the ball downward by making contact with the top half of the ball
- If heading to defend, head the ball upward by making contact with the lower half of the ball
- Always follow through with the head and upper body in the direction that you want the ball to go

Heading Exercises and Games

Use the following exercises and games (described in detail in Chapter 13) to develop heading skills:

- Zoo Time **51**
- Crossing the River **52**
- Head Catch Juggling **53**
- Heading Races **54**
- Heads Up **55**
- Partner Head Catch **56**
- Heading Wars **57**
- Two-on-Two Heading **58**
- Attacking Headers **59**
- Throw, Head, Catch **60**

Coaching Advice

"Like many techniques, heading must be taught in a progressive manner. A 7-year-old will not just magically be able to score with her head from a cross. The most important element with young girls is to build their confidence in heading the ball."

Common Problems and Corrections

Problem: When a girl is heading for the goal, the ball doesn't have sufficient power. **Correction:** It's a common mistake with young players to just get in position and let the ball hit the head. The girl must generate power by using her legs, arms, upper body, and neck to attack through the ball.

Problem: The ball is headed over the top of the goal. **Correction:** Contact was made underneath the ball or with the top of the head. This is common when a player closes her eyes at the last moment. She must keep her eyes open and jump if necessary to get above the top half of the ball, heading downward through the ball.

Problem: The girl is afraid she'll get hit in the face. **Correction:** Build confidence by teaching heading in a progressive manner. Encourage the girl to keep her eyes open throughout so she can see where the ball is.

Problem: My players complain of headaches when we practice heading. **Correction:** There's no evidence to support the statement that heading can cause brain or head injury, but practicing heading infrequently for extended periods at a time and using soccer balls that are either too big or too hard will give anybody a headache. Practice heading on a regular basis for 10–15 minutes. Use soccer balls that are the correct size for the age of your girls.

Problem: When defending corners the girls can't clear the ball. **Correction:** The ball must be headed away from the goal. Aim high and wide, clearing the ball out from dangerous areas of the field and away from the opposing attackers. With defensive headers a player must use her legs to spring up through the ball, giv-

Stages of heading. The knees and waist are bent in preparation to head the ball (1).

The arms and body are used to thrust the neck and forehead through the ball (2).

It's important to keep the eyes open throughout and use the forehead to head the ball (3).

Coaching Advice

"Encourage the girls to keep their eyes open when heading and to follow through the ball using their head, neck, and back. This follow-through should be in the direction they want the ball to go."

Progressive Heading for Girls.

- **Hand feed:** Each girl holds a ball in her hands level with her head and heads the ball forward out of her hands using her forehead. Emphasize keeping the eyes on the ball.
- **Self-feed:** Each girl throws the ball up in the air just above her head and uses her forehead to head the ball back up and catch it.

- **Catch headers:** Challenge each girl to do one header and catch the ball. Next she does two consecutive headers and catches the ball. Then she does three headers, four headers, and finally five headers. If the ball hits the ground, she must start from the beginning.
- **Head to partner:** To develop power in the heading technique, each girl now throws the ball up in the air and heads the ball to a partner about 5 yards away.
- **Kneeling partner feed:** In pairs on their knees, one girl feeds the ball gently underarm so that her partner can head it back.
- **Standing partner feed:** In pairs, one girl feeds the ball gently underarm so that her partner can head it back. As the girls develop their ability and confidence, increase the distance between the two players and work on defensive and offensive headers.

Defending Exercises and Games

Use the following exercises and games (described in detail in Chapters 12, 13, and 15) to teach the technique of defending:

Defending

When the opposition has possession, a team must defend its goal and try to win the ball back. The technique used to do this is *defending*. Although some players don't consider it as glamorous and exciting as shooting and finishing, defending is equally as important. Defending occurs every time the opponent has the ball, and players defend individually, in small groups, and as a team. The technique of individual defending involves denying space and time to attackers and winning back possession of the ball.

How to Teach Defending.

- Close down the attacker's space by sprinting toward the player with the ball as quickly as possible
- As you get closer to the attacker, slow down and adopt the defensive stance; the distance will be determined by the experience and the ability of both the defender and attacker (start with 3 to 4 yards). In a defensive stance similar to surfing, position the body sideways, on the balls of the feet, with the knees bent and arms out for balance
- Always keep the eyes focused on the ball
- Maintain the distance from the ball by shuffling backward in the defensive stance
- Avoid crossing the feet
- If the attacker moves to one side, pivot on the back foot
- Be patient—don't dive in

Patience is vital when defending. Often when the attacker is pressured and denied space, she'll lose control of the ball and give it away. If the defender recognizes that control has been lost, she should step in and take possession of the ball.

Tackling

While the attacker still has the ball under control, the defender must remain patient and try to win the ball by *tackling*, or using the feet to take away the ball. Players must learn not only how to tackle but also when to tackle. If the timing of the tackle is incorrect, then the defender will be caught off balance and unable to prevent the attacker from moving toward the goal.

A tackle should be made if the attacker hesitates, temporarily loses control of the ball, or attempts to dribble past the defender. It should occur when the chances of winning the ball are high. The tackle can be made with either the toe or the inside of the foot while in the defensive stance.

How to Teach Tackling.

- Using the toe of the front foot, poke the ball away from the attacker in between her touches
- With the inside of the back foot, lean forward and step into the ball just before the attacker takes a touch
- Follow through the ball after making contact

Common Problems and Corrections

Problem: Whenever one girl makes a tackle, she still gets beaten by the attacker. **Correction:** This is a common problem with young players and can be attributed to timing. Teach the girl to be patient and to recognize the signs of when to step in and make the tackle.

Coaching Advice

"It's common for young girls to initially tackle tentatively. They must learn to tackle aggressively and develop a mentality that they must win the ball back for the team. This comes by building confidence in their defensive abilities, so encourage and praise them when they tackle aggressively, even if their technique isn't perfect. If they have the right mentality, then the technique can be improved."

CHAPTER 8

Goalkeeping

Goalkeeping Exercises and Games

Use the following exercises and games (described in detail in Chapters 13 and 14) to develop goalkeeping techniques:

- Rapid Fire **44**
- Street Soccer **45**
- One-on-One to the Goal **49**
- Around the World II **61**
- Handling Races **62**
- Home Alone **63**
- One-on-One Diving **64**
- Keeper Rapid Fire **65**
- Keeper Wars **66**
- Drive Back **67**
- Numbered Saves **68**
- 10 Wins **69**

As the goalkeeper is the only player who can use her hands, she requires special techniques and training.

The goalkeeper is possibly the single most important position on the team, as she's responsible for preventing the ball from going in the goal. At an early age all girls must be given the opportunity to learn to play in goal so they all develop confidence in this position. Goalkeeping is a specialist position, and because the goalkeeper is the only player on the field who can use her hands, the position requires special techniques, skills, and rules to learn. Techniques include catching the ball, blocking shots, diving, and punting. Goalkeepers must be given the opportunity to get a feel for the ball and to become a master of the ball using their hands. Handling skills should be practiced as often as possible.

Although it's frequently the hands that prevent the goal, it's important to remember that the feet must position the body to get in line with the ball and to prepare the body to jump, dive, and make the save. Developing good footwork is essential with female goalkeepers. Once you've identified a small group of players who will regularly play in goal, it's important that they get the chance to practice their handling and footwork skills on a regular basis. These girls must master goalkeeping techniques as well as participate in the regular practices to learn and develop the basic soccer skills along with all the other girls.

Additional Equipment

As goalkeepers can use their hands to catch the ball and make saves, it's common and advisable for them to wear keeper gloves. As they progress to developing diving skills, padded shirts and shorts should be worn to provide additional protection. Before the age of 10 some leagues may choose to have goalkeepers wear padded helmets during games to protect against head injuries. If nothing else, it gives the girl in the goal a sense of being protected, leading to more confidence when coming out of the net and collecting balls.

The starting position allows the goalkeeper to react and make a save in any direction (top).

With the correct scooping technique, the feet are together, and both legs are behind the ball (bottom).

Starting Position

The goalkeeper's starting position is essential because a balanced, ready position is necessary for moving quickly and reacting in any direction. The goalkeeper should prepare herself by doing the following:

- Stand on the balls of the feet
- Position the feet approximately shoulder width apart
- Place the hands at waist height to the side of the body
- Turn the palms of the hands facing out
- Hold the head steady

Catching at Ground

Balls on the ground or close to the ground can be caught from either a scooping position or from a kneeling position.

Scooping Technique.

- Get the entire body behind the path of the ball
- Move the feet close together so the ball won't go through the legs if a mistake is made
- Position the hands low to the ground with the fingers pointed down and the palms facing the ball
- Extend the arms out so that the hands meet the ball as early as possible
- Use the hands to scoop the ball into the body
- Wrap the arms under and around the ball to make it secure

Kneeling Technique.

- Get the entire body behind the path of the ball
- Turn the right foot 90° and bend both legs to kneel on the left leg

- Position the left knee in front of the right ankle so that it's impossible for the ball to go through the legs if a mistake is made
- Position the upper body so that it faces the ball throughout
- Use the hands to scoop the ball into the body
- Wrap the arms under and around the ball to make it secure

Catching at Height

Balls may be caught at several heights. The main emphasis on all should be getting in line with the flight of the ball.

With the correct kneeling technique, the upper body remains facing the ball throughout.

Waist-Height Catching Technique.

- Move the feet so the body is balanced and positioned behind the flight of the ball
- Position the hands with the fingers pointing outward and the palms facing upward
- Extend the arms to catch the ball as early as possible
- Keep the elbows tucked in
- Reach out with the hands and pull the ball up into the body
- Wrap the forearms around the front of the ball to secure it against the chest

Catching at waist height: extend the arms and hands to meet the ball (left).

The ball is secured by pulling it into the chest (right).

With the correct catching technique, a chest-height ball is caught with the hands in front of the body. The ball must be caught with the hands positioned from the middle to the top of the ball as opposed to the lower half of the ball. If the hands are positioned at the lower half of the ball, the ball is more likely to slide past/slip off the fingers (left).

With the correct trapping technique, the hands are used to guide the ball into the chest (right).

There are two basic techniques used when the ball is at chest height. It can either be caught or trapped with the chest.

Chest-Height Catching Technique.

- Move the feet so the body is balanced and positioned behind the flight of the ball
- Position the hands in front of chest with the palms facing outward and the fingers pointing upward
- Catch the ball as early as possible with the pads of the fingers
- Catch the top half of the ball
- Cushion the ball using the arms
- Secure the ball into the chest by moving the hands around the ball and pulling it into the body

Chest-Height Trapping Technique.

- Use the feet to position the entire body in line with the flight of the ball
- Position the hands with the palms facing inward and the fingers pointing upward
- Lean forward to get the head and shoulders over the ball
- Use the hands to guide the ball into the chest
- Wrap the forearms around the front of the ball, securing it against the chest

Catching a ball above the head. Notice how the thumbs are together and the fingers spread apart (1).

Good foot movement is important so that the body is positioned behind the ball when it's caught (2).

Goalkeepers must be encouraged to jump and catch the ball at the highest possible point (3).

Catching the Ball above the Head. The following technique is used for catching a ball that is above the keeper's head:

- Move the feet so the body is balanced and positioned in line with the flight of the ball
- Position the hands above the head with the palms out, fingers spread, and thumbs together
- Catch the ball as high and as early as possible with the pads of the fingers

Common Problems and Corrections

Problem: The ball keeps going past the goalkeeper's body into the goal. **Correction:** If the ball is to the girl's left, she's probably trying to make the save by just moving her arms and hands out to the left and trying to catch it. Make sure she uses her feet to position herself in line with the ball. If the ball is to her left, she must move her whole body to the left so that when she catches the ball her whole body is behind it.

Problem: When the keeper tries to catch the ball, it bounces off her hands. **Correction:** The ball is hitting the palms of the hands, which have no give. The girl must use the tips of her fingers to catch the ball and use both her fingers and arms to cushion it.

Problem: The keeper has difficulty catching the ball at waist height. **Correction:** As the position of the hands and fingers changes depending on the height of the ball, it's not uncommon for keepers to get confused over which technique to use when the ball is in the mid zone. The palms should be facing upward, with the fingers pointing outward. Encourage the player to extend her arms and pull the ball into

- If necessary jump off the ground to catch the ball at its highest point
- Pull the ball down into the body
- Wrap the forearms around the front of the ball, securing it against the chest

Diving

Just as Olympic platform divers don't begin diving from the highest platform, you shouldn't expect your beginning goalkeepers to make diving saves up into the top corner of the goal. Diving must be taught in a progressive manner to develop both confidence and the correct technique. Building confidence with female goalkeepers at an early age is essential in their development.

Progressive Diving for Female Goalkeepers.

- **Sitting position:** Each girl is seated on the ground and attempts to roll the ball past a teammate into a small goal about 5 yards away. The girl receiving the ball must be seated in the middle of her goal and must stretch (dive) to her side to prevent the ball from going in. Roles are then reversed, and the girl receiving the ball rolls it to the other girl.
- **Kneeling position:** Once the goalkeepers are comfortable stretching and falling to the side, have them dive from a kneeling position. Emphasize proper body, arm, and hand positioning.
- **Crouching position:** Make the goals slightly bigger, and have the partner roll the ball from further away. The save is now made from a crouching position, which allows for further development of the diving technique. Footwork can be introduced along with collapsing and extending the body.
- **Standing position:** Increase the size of the goal and have each goalkeeper make her dive from a standing position. Further develop the goalkeepers' collapsing technique and footwork. Finally, vary the serves and distance from goal. Introduce diving saves in the air.

How to Teach the Diving Technique.

- Push out and off to the side using the foot nearest the ball—don't dive backward
- Keep the body facing outward throughout the dive
- Keep the eyes on the ball
- Fully extend the lower arm to make the save, using the lower hand

Special Note on Footwork

The full-size soccer goal was designed for the male athlete. With less muscle mass, female goalkeepers are unable to dive as high or as far as their male counterparts, leaving a larger area of the goal vulnerable. Developing good positioning and footwork is therefore essential for female goalkeepers.

Diving. Whether the ball is on the ground or in the air, diving saves are exciting to perform and exciting to watch (1).

The body should remain facing outward throughout the save (2).

The lower hand is positioned behind the ball, and the upper hand is on top (3).

- Position the lower hand behind the ball and bring upper hand on top of the ball
- Land on the side of the body and use the upper leg to stabilize the body, preventing it from rolling over
- Secure the ball by pulling it into the chest and wrapping the forearms around the front of the ball

How to Teach the Collapsing Technique. When the shots are low to the ground, to the side of the goal-keeper and moving too fast for the body to move behind the path of the ball, a collapsing technique must be used to make the save.

- Keep the eyes on the ball
- Bend and collapse the leg nearest to the ball
- Collapse the leg from underneath the body
- Allow the body to drop quickly to the ground
- Position the lower hand behind the ball and bring the upper hand on top of the ball
- Land on the side of the body and use the upper leg to stabilize the body, preventing it from rolling over
- Secure the ball by pulling it into the chest and wrapping the forearms around the front of the ball

Collapsing technique. The leg nearest the ball bends and collapses underneath the body (1).

The lower hand moves to get behind the ball, and the upper hand moves on top of the ball (2).

The keeper lands on her side and uses the upper leg to stabilize her body (3).

Additional Goalkeeper Techniques

Punching Technique

If the ball is above the head but too high to catch, then it should be punched clear. Encourage the goalkeeper to punch the ball with two fists. The punch should be through the bottom half of the ball. She should aim to clear the ball as high and as far away as possible.

Narrowing the Angle

One of the most important techniques to both understand and master in order to stop shots on goal is that of narrowing the angle. The goalkeeper must be taught to minimize the size of the open goal at which the attacker can aim.

How to Teach Narrowing the Angle.

- Keep positioned in a line between the ball and the midpoint of the goal, minimizing the distance side to side that needs to be covered
- As the ball moves, maintain this position by adjusting the body
- Shuffle the feet, keeping them approximately shoulder width apart

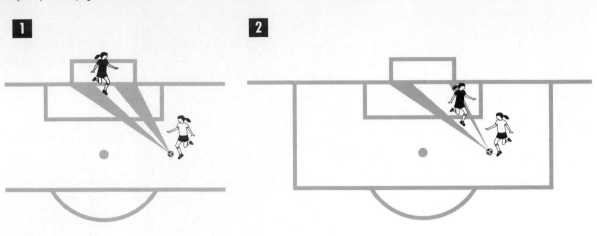

Narrowing the angle.
Incorrect position (1).

Correct position (2).

- Don't let the feet come too close together or cross over
- Reduce the shooting area by advancing quickly off the goal line toward the ball, which increases the area of the goal that is covered
- Avoid advancing too far out of the goal, to avoid becoming vulnerable to a chipped shot—the distance to advance depends on the position and ability of the attacker with the ball
- Get in the starting position to be ready and balanced to make the save

Communication

The goalkeeper isn't just the shot stopper; she's an integral part of the entire defensive unit, providing both support and communication for the other members. She has an important responsibility to organize her teammates and communicate what's going on. Goalkeepers must be encouraged to communicate to the team and be taught to do so in a clear, concise, and calm manner.

Distribution

Once the ball is in her hands, the goalkeeper is no longer the last line of defense. She's the first line of attack and must distribute the ball to a teammate by a kick, throw, or roll. It's important to stress to the goalkeeper that her distribution must enable the team to maintain possession of the ball and not give it away.

With a young goalkeeper, encourage her to run to the edge of the penalty area and roll the ball quickly to an open player. The ball should be released underarm so that it stays on the ground and is easier for the receiving player to control.

Rolling the ball. For the ball to be rolled with sufficient speed, take several run-up steps, swing back the throwing arm first and then follow through as the ball is released (1, 2).

How to Teach Rolling the Ball.

- Holding the ball securely, take several run-up steps in the direction of the target player
- Point the nonthrowing arm in the direction of the target player
- From a crouching position, swing back the throwing arm
- In one smooth motion, swing the arm forward as if bowling
- Release the ball as the arm goes past the front leg
- Follow through in the direction of the target player

The ball is released as the arm goes past the front leg.

If the open player is slightly farther away, the ball must be thrown overhand. The flight of the ball should be direct with no arc and no backspin.

How to Teach the Overarm Throw.

- Take several run-up steps in the direction of the target player
- Point the nonthrowing arm in the direction of the target player
- Aim the ball so it lands at the teammate's feet
- Hold the ball with the fingertips and hand
- Keeping the throwing arm straight, pull the ball from waist height up and over the shoulder

Overarm throw. The ball is pulled from behind the body, with the throwing arm kept straight (1, 2).

The ball is released as the arm passes the ear (3).

- Release the ball as the arm moves forward and passes the ear
- Follow through down and across the body

If no throwing options are open or if the available teammates are too far away to be reached by a throw, the ball should be kicked from the hands.

How to Teach Punting.

- Position the ball in front of the body
- Take several steps, run in the direction of the target player, and drop the ball for a low volley
- Keep the head down and the eyes focused on the ball
- Lock the ankle and strike the ball with the instep (lace)
- Follow through above the waist

Punting. The ball is released in front of the body as the punting leg is pulled back (1).

The ball is struck using the instep (2).

The goalkeeper's punting leg follows through above her waist (3).

Common Problems and Corrections

Problem: When the goalkeeper rolls out the ball, it's frequently intercepted by the opposition. **Correction:** The rolling technique should be used only if a player is open and fairly close to the keeper. If, when rolling the ball, the throwing arm stops as the swing reaches the body, very little power is transferred through the ball. Encourage the girl to follow through with the arm.

Problem: When the keeper kicks the ball, she's unable to make it go straight. **Correction:** When contact is made on the side of the ball or off center, it won't go in the desired direction. Make sure the keeper is kicking through the middle of the ball. Encourage her to watch her foot make contact with the ball.

Essential Tactics

As soon as opponents and teammates are introduced into games and practices, each girl must make decisions about what to do. Tactics are those decisions players must make offensively, defensively, with the ball, and without the ball. The game of soccer involves a series of individual and group tactical situations, with each player literally making hundreds of decisions, usually with very little time to think.

Offensive tactics are used when your team has the ball. Girls must decide what techniques to use where and when in order to maintain possession, beat defenders, and create goal-scoring opportunities.

Defensive tactics are used when the opposition has the ball. Girls must decide where to position themselves so as to prevent their opponents from penetrating. They must decide when the best opportunity is to win back possession of the ball, when to make a tackle, and when to follow attacking runs.

Tactical decisions must occur individually, in small groups, and as an entire team. Tactical awareness increases with mental development, age, and experience, so it's important that players under the age of 13 are frequently put in decision-making situations. As offensive tactics require an ability to perform technically while under pressure, and defensive tactics are more focused on positioning, considerable emphasis should be placed on developing tactics in attacking situations. Wherever possible, set up practices and games that develop your team both technically and tactically at the same time.

Offensive Tactics

Individual Offensive Tactics

Individual tactics are those decisions a girl who has the ball must make in order to create space on the field. Tactically should she pass, dribble, or shoot?

If she's going to dribble, where should her first touch go, and what move will she use to beat the defender?

When to Dribble. Deciding when to dribble depends on several factors, including where on the field a player is, how much space and time she has, where defenders are positioned, and what passing options are available. Generally, if the play is in the attacking third and there's space behind the defender, she should look to take on that defender. The reward of beating the defender and creating a goal-scoring opportunity is greater than the risk of losing possession and conceding a goal. If, however, the same situation occurs in the defensive third, then the risk outweighs the reward. Girls should generally be encouraged to dribble in the attacking third and maintain possession by passing in the defensive third.

    Creating one-on-one competition is the most effective way of developing individual tactics as each girl is continuously forced to make decisions. An attacker with the ball must quickly decide when and how to beat a defender and must also learn to adapt her decisions as a situation develops. One-on-one competition is the most economical way of having your team practice technically and tactically at the same time.

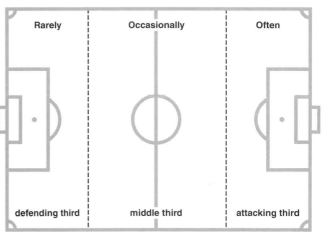

Where to dribble on the soccer field.

How to Develop Individual Offensive Tactics.

- Recognize when the time is right to take on defenders
- If there's space behind the defender, dribble and take her on
- If the defender is covered or there's no space in which to penetrate, look to maintain possession
- Have a positive attitude and don't hesitate when dribbling and taking on defenders
- Before taking on the defender, decide which side to attack her on
- Decide what move to perform to get her off balance
- Recognize when to take the ball quickly in the desired direction
- Accelerate into the space behind the defender

Attacking Principles

Whether your team is playing a small-sided game or the 11-on-11 game, the objective of soccer is to move the ball upfield, maintain possession, and score a goal. In order to create space and do this successfully, four basic attacking principles are required. Understanding these principles will help your girls develop good tactical awareness.

Penetration. Girls must penetrate with the ball into space behind defenders either by dribbling or passing. Creating space through width, depth, and mobility in attack is essential in order to penetrate.

Depth. Players must provide support and passing options ahead and behind the girl with the ball. To maximize depth in attack, forwards should provide options as far up the field as possible. When the forwards are able to force the opposition toward their own goal, they create space for themselves to move back into and also space in which the girl with the ball can attack by dribbling or passing.

Width. Players must provide passing options on either side of the ball, so that the ball can be switched from side to side and the opposition can be stretched apart and become unbalanced, creating space between defenders.

Mobility. Players must force defenders to move out of good defensive positions by making runs off the ball. Diagonal runs across the field and runs up and down the field force defenders to make quick decisions and to be pulled out of position, creating space.

Small-Group Offensive Tactics

During a soccer game the team in possession must attempt to create space in which to penetrate—that is, move the ball forward into the space behind defenders—either through individual dribbling or by several players combining together. The manner in which players combine to create space and penetrate involves small-group tactics. The simplest of these tactics involves just two attacking players, the girl with the ball, who is the *first attacker*, and the supporting teammate, who is the *second attacker*.

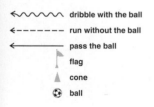

→〜〜〜〜 dribble with the ball
←------- run without the ball
←——— pass the ball
🚩 flag
▲ cone
⚽ ball

How to Teach the Wall Pass. The wall pass is used when a supporting teammate is ahead of the ball, providing support to the side, for a quick pass around the defender into space.

- The first attacker (X_1) dribbles at the defender, drawing her into the ball
- X_1 dribbles at an angle away from her supporting teammate (X_2), rather than toward her
- X_2, who is ahead of the ball, provides support for a pass at an angle and distance far enough away that the defender is unable to cover both passing and dribbling options

The wall pass.

- X_1 disguises the pass by playing the ball while in her natural running stride—a pass with the outside of the foot is harder for the defender to anticipate than a pass with the inside
- X_1 passes to the feet of X_2 and sprints into the space behind the defender to receive the return pass
- X_2 immediately makes a return pass to X_1 in the space behind the defender
- If the defender shifts toward X_2 to cover the initial pass, X_1 attacks into the space by dribbling herself

How to Teach the Overlap. An overlap is used when the supporting player comes from behind the player with the ball. The overlapping player can cause defenders to be pulled out of position, creating space for the girl with the ball to dribble or providing a passing option forward into space. Overlaps often occur on the sides of the field when girls from defensive positions overlap teammates farther up the field.

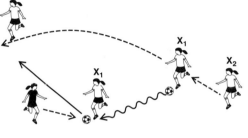

- The first attacker (X_1) dribbles toward the defender, drawing her into the ball
- The second attacker (X_2) behind the ball communicates that she's making an overlapping run that continues behind the player with the ball beyond the defender
- X_1 passes the ball forward into the space ahead of where her teammate is making the overlapping run
- If the defender shifts to cover the pass or is pulled off balance by the overlap, X_1 can attack into the space by dribbling

The overlap.

How to Teach the Takeover. A takeover is used when the supporting player comes toward the ball, crossing over in front of the defender. It's great for pulling defenders out of tight spaces.

- The first attacker (X_1) dribbles toward her teammate, X_2, using the outside of her foot
- X_1 uses the foot farthest away from the defender so that her body screens the ball
- X_2 simultaneously moves toward X_1
- X_1 communicates with X_2 so that they both know who will take the ball when they cross over
- If the defender is moving in the same direction as X_1, X_2 takes over control of the ball, using the outside of the foot nearest the ball as they cross over
- If the defender shifts direction to anticipate a takeover, X_1 fakes and continues with the ball

The takeover.

- Both players accelerate away after they've crossed over so the defender is unsure of who has the ball

How to Teach the Double Pass. The double pass is used when the supporting player is ahead of the ball and is being marked closely. Space is created behind a defender by the attacker drawing the defender into the ball and then quickly turning to receive a pass behind her.

- The second attacker (X_2) makes a run at an angle toward the ball, bringing the defender with her and pulling her out of position
- The first attacker (X_1) passes the ball to X_2, who immediately plays it back
- X_2 turns and runs forward into the space behind the defender
- X_1 plays a one-touch pass into this space for X_2

The double pass.

Defensive Tactics

When a team doesn't have the ball, the players must attempt to win back possession and prevent the opposition from scoring. The main objective will depend on where the ball is on the field. When the ball is in front of a team's goal, the primary role is to stop the opponents from scoring. When the ball is at the other end of the field, the objective is to win back possession of the ball. Decisions on defending individually, in small groups, and as a team in different areas of the field are defensive tactics.

Defensive Principles

Four basic principles are required in order to defend successfully. These are very much the opposite of the attacking principles. Understanding how they relate to the game will help your players develop good tactical awareness.

Delay. The movement of the opposition up the field must be slowed down and delayed by denying space immediately in front of the ball. Delaying the attack gives time for players to get back between the ball and the goal and allows the defense to get compact and organized. It's the responsibility of the girl closest to the ball to initially delay the attacking team by quickly pressuring the player with the ball. This girl is called the *first defender.*

Depth. Defensive players must provide cover behind the ball by positioning themselves between the ball and the goal. The girl pressuring the ball must have cover behind her, so that if she's beaten, the attacker can't just go straight to the goal. With depth in the defense, the attacker is pressured a second time by one of the covering defenders and is prevented from going to the goal. It's a major responsibility of the *second defender* to provide depth in defense.

Balance. Players behind the ball must ensure the defense is balanced by covering the space into which runs and penetrating passes are made. This space is covered by defenders positioning themselves in relation to attackers and the ball. To provide good balance in defense, girls must be able to see the ball and the offensive player for whom they're directly responsible. The closer an attacker is to the ball, the tighter she must be marked. If an attacker is farther away from the ball, the defending player doesn't need to mark so tightly and instead can position herself closer toward the goal.

Balanced defending. Defenders X_3 and X_4 balance the defense by covering the space in which runs and penetrating passes could be made.

Compactness. Defending players must limit the space and time for attackers by reducing the space between each other and remaining compact, which prevents the opposition from penetrating with passes through or over the defense. As the opposition spreads wide on the field, the entire defense must shift as a unit to maintain this compactness. When the attack is down one side of the field, players on the opposite side must shift toward the middle of the field. If the attack is central, players must position themselves toward the middle of the field, denying space and time in front of goal.

Individual Defensive Tactics

One-on-one situations provide the best opportunity to learn and develop individual defensive tactics. Defenders must decide where and how close to the attacker to position themselves, which side to make the attacker play, how long to delay the attacker, and when to tackle and win the ball. One-on-one competition is the most economical way of developing defensive technique and tactics at the same time.

Initial Positioning. The defender must always take up a position between the ball and the goal she's defending. This is called being *goal side*. Whenever possession is lost, the defender must retreat back so that she is goal side.

Pressuring Distance. When a defender is closing down the attacker with the ball, the decision on how close to pressure varies depending on the ability of the attacker, the ability of the defender, and the location of the ball on the field. If the attacker is fast and well skilled, this distance should be increased.

If the attacker is less skilled, then the defender can pressure more closely. Similarly, if a defender is good and self-confident, then she can pressure much closer. If there's limited space on the field that the attacker can use to beat the defender, then the pressure can be closer to the ball. This distance will continuously change as players learn and make decisions based on their previous experience.

Where to Pressure. Should the defender pressure the attacker, forcing her to play to her left or her right, the inside or the outside? These decisions are based on the area of the field and the ability of both players. In the defensive third of the field, the defender should force the attacker away from the goal, so that she's unable to take a shot. If the attacker is in the middle of the field, then she should be forced to the side of her weaker foot. If the attacker is by the sideline, then the defender can use the lack of space to her advantage by forcing the attacker to the outside.

Where to Retreat. Retreat toward the goal as opposed to the goal line. Players playing wide should retreat back and to the middle of the field. Players playing near the center of the field should retreat back toward the goal.

Be Patient. The best defenders in the world are those who are patient. The timing of the tackle is essential. If mistimed, the defender will overcommit or will be off balance and easily beaten. Patience delays the attack, allowing time for teammates to make recovery runs. When an attacker is pressured, it's not uncommon for her to make mistakes and lose control of the ball, allowing for the defender to win back possession without ever making a tackle.

Group Defending

When more than one player is involved in defending, the tactics and decisions that are involved vary from player to player based on each girl's position relative to the ball and the attackers. The girl nearest the attacker with the ball is referred to as the *first defender*.

First Defender. It's the first defender's responsibility to do the following:

- Close down and pressure the attacker with the ball
- Prevent the attacker from penetrating forward
- Delay the attack, allowing time for her teammates to recover and get goal side
- Make play predictable for other defending teammates by making a curved run and forcing the attacker to play in a desired direction

The first defender's decisions are the same as those mentioned in individual defensive tactics, except they're now also influenced by the support, positioning, and communication of her teammates. If she has covering de-

---

Coaching Advice

"Explain to parents the importance of being patient when defending. Parents will often be heard shouting on the sideline for the girl nearest the ball to go win or take the ball immediately. This may cause her to dive in and make a mistimed tackle instead of being patient, delaying the attack, and waiting for the correct time to win back the ball."

fenders on her right side and only space to her left, she'll force the attacker to play in the direction of this support. With a covering player behind her, she can decide to put greater pressure on the attacker with the ball. This covering player, who is close to the ball but isn't actually pressuring, is known as the *second defender*.

Second Defender. It's the second defender's responsibility to do the following:

- Provide cover for the first defender. If the first defender is beaten, the second defender must be close enough to deny any further penetration by putting pressure on the attacker with the ball.
- Communicate and give information to the first defender. The second defender must let her teammate know that she's there providing cover and must instruct her where to force the attacker with the ball.
- Cover any pass to a second attacker. If the ball is passed, the second defender must be positioned at an angle and distance that allow her to immediately put pressure on the ball and delay the attack from moving forward.
- Track the runs of the second attacker. If the second attacker makes a run forward ahead of the ball or from one side to the other, the second defender must track these runs while still providing cover for her teammate.

Communication: It's important when defending that players know who's going to pressure and provide cover and also where to pressure and cover. Girls must communicate who they're marking and which offensive runs they're covering. This communication must be encouraged from an early age.

Positioning: The second defender must be positioned goal side, at an angle behind the first defender and to the side. A good starting angle is 45° to the side. The decision on how far behind and how far to the side depends on how much pressure is on the ball, the location of the second attacker on the field, and the location of the ball. If the second defender is positioned level with the first defender, then there's no depth in the defense, and she's no longer able to provide cover if her teammate should be beaten. If the second defender is directly behind the first defender, then she would be unable to cover a pass to the second attacker.

Distance: If there's a lot of pressure on the ball, and the play is being forced away from the second attacker, then this defender can be much closer to her teammate. Players must learn to recognize when such opportunities exist and whether there's an opportunity to double-team the attacker with the ball. If there's less pressure on the ball and the possibility for a pass exists, the second defender must be farther behind and to the side. She must be at an angle and distance that allow her to cover both her teammate and the pass. The closer the ball is to the goal, the closer the second defender should be to the first defender.

Tracking: If the second attacker makes a run from one side of the ball to the other, then the second defender must track this run by moving and providing cover on the other side of her teammate. At all times she must make sure she's providing cover for the first defender. The second defender must also track any forward runs made by this attacker ahead of the ball. How far to track these runs will depend on the support from the balancing defenders and whether the run is being made into an offside position. Once again the defender must make sure she's providing cover for the first defender. As the attacking situation is always changing, the position and decisions of the second defender must also change. Players must develop tactically through practice so that their decisions and positioning become automatic based on what they see.

Third Defender. Any girl who's not pressuring the ball or providing immediate cover near the ball must provide the defense with balance. This is the *third defender*. In a team there can be several players at any one time providing balance. It's their primary responsibility to do the following:

- Cover all penetrating passes
- Track all penetrating runs

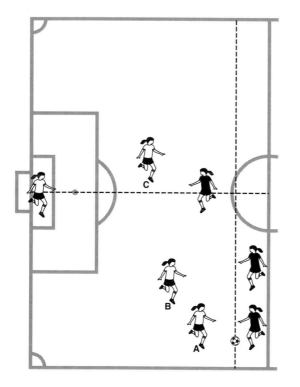 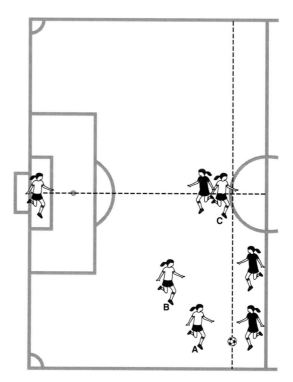

Incorrect positioning for the third defender: Player C isn't ball side of her mark. She isn't between the ball and the girl she's marking.

Incorrect positioning for the third defender: Player C isn't goal side of her mark. She isn't between the goal and the girl she's marking.

Positioning: The third defenders must be positioned goal side and ball side. This means they must be between the attacker they're marking and the goal and between the attacker and the ball.

Distance: The closer the attacker is to the ball, the tighter she must be marked. If an attacker is some distance from the ball, the defender can mark her less closely and can be positioned in more toward the goal. The distance of the third defender from the attacker also depends on whether the attacker she's marking is able to receive a pass. This is determined by the pressure and angle of the first defender. If the attacker is able to receive a pass, the third defender must mark her more closely. If she's unable to receive the pass, the third defender can mark less closely and once again be positioned in more toward the goal.

Tracking: The third defenders must pick up and track attackers as they run across the field and toward the goal. How far the runs are tracked depends on the distance from the goal, whether the run is made in front of the ball, and whether the run is likely to lead to a penetrating pass. Good communication is essential so that the defenders know who's tracking each attacker. To avoid being pulled out of position by attacking runs, defenders must communicate so they can switch the players they're marking. The closer the ball and the attackers are to the goal, the closer the runs must be tracked by each individual defender. The balancing defenders must use their knowledge of the offside rule to avoid tracking attackers who run behind the last defender into offside positions.

Recovery runs: When a team losses possession, the defender nearest the ball must delay the attack to allow her teammates time to get back into good defensive positions. The runs made to get back into these defensive positions are called *recovery runs*. Girls who are in wide positions

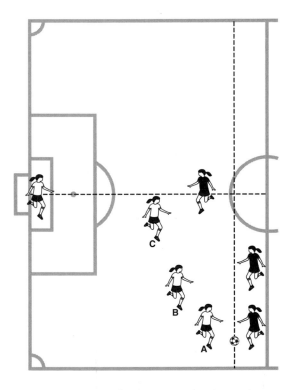

Correct positioning for the third defender: Player C is ball side and goal side. She's positioned between her mark and the ball and between her mark and the goal.

should make recovery runs back in a line toward the goal post closest to them, and girls who are in central positions should make recovery runs back toward the center of the goal. These recovery runs must be made quickly and as soon as possession of the ball is lost.

Possession Tactics

When a player with the ball is pressured, she must quickly decide how best to maintain possession of the ball: She must choose by dribbling, shielding, or passing the ball. Each of these different techniques involves a variety of important tactical decisions.

Who and Where to Pass To? If a girl decides to pass the ball to maintain possession, she must also decide which teammate to pass to. Girls must learn when to pass forward, when to pass backward, when to play long passes, when to pass to a teammate's feet, and when to pass into space. To make these tactical decisions, players must assess the entire field, looking at the position of the opposition and their teammates. They must take into account their own technical ability, the score of the game, and their position on the field.

If possession can be maintained passing forward, do so. If possession can't be maintained with a forward pass, the next choice is to pass sideways. If possession can't be maintained with a sideways pass, then look to pass backward. If there's no passing option and the player is unable to dribble, then she must temporarily protect the ball with her body until a teammate gets open for a pass. This is called *shielding*.

Pass Forward or Backward? The objective of the game is to move the ball into the other team's goal, so players should attempt to pass the ball forward whenever possible. If there's a teammate open ahead of the ball and another teammate open behind the ball, and there are no other factors to consider, the girl with the ball should pass forward. If the player ahead of the ball is too far away for the pass to be played accurately and maintain possession, then the girl should pass backward.

Pass to the Left or Right? If the girl with the ball is in the middle of the field when pressured by the opposition, and she has two unmarked teammates ahead of her, then her decision is also influenced by the position of the defenders. If there are two defenders on her right and one on her left, then she should pass to the girl on her left, creating an attacking one-on-one situation.

Pass to Feet or Space? To decide whether to pass to feet or into space, a player must take into account the position of the marking defender. If a teammate is marked closely, the pass should be into space because a pass to feet gives the defender an opportunity to intercept. If there's space behind the defender where the teammate can make a run and receive the ball, then a penetrating pass into space can be played. If there's little space behind the defender, and the defender isn't too close to the teammate, then the pass should be played to her feet.

Score and Field Position. The score of the game and the position on the field can influence the passing decision. When there isn't much time left to play, the team that's behind may choose to attempt riskier penetrating passes in the hope of being rewarded with a goal-scoring opportunity. In contrast, the team that's ahead can afford to just maintain possession of the ball and look to penetrate less often. When playing penetrating passes, greater risks can be taken in the attacking third of the field; if possession of the ball is lost, there's no immediate threat of conceding a goal.

Developing Possession Tactics

The simplest way to teach and develop the decision making involved in maintaining possession of the ball is through small games of Keep-Away (see Game 21 on page 146). Once players are able to keep possession based on the position and pressure of defenders through games such as three-on-one and four-on-two, a purpose and direction should be added to the game so that players develop an understanding of penetrating while maintaining possession.

Three-on-One Possession. In this possession game, girls improve passing and first touch, while continuously making game-like tactical decisions. They must decide who to pass to, what kind of pass to play, the weight of the pass, when to pass, how to disguise the pass, what runs to make in order to provide support for a pass, and where to control the ball. All these decisions are based on the position of the defender, availability of supporting teammates, and available time and space.

- Pass to the teammate who has the most space and time
- Keep the direction of the pass secret by positioning the body open to the field of play, allowing for a pass in either supporting direction
- Disguise the pass by pretending to play in one direction and then, while the defender is off balance, pass in the opposite direction
- Commit the defender in to the ball—i.e., get the defender to move in the direction of the ball—before passing, creating more time and space for teammates
- Play the pass with the correct weight so the ball reaches the teammate quickly but at a speed she is able to control
- When receiving the pass, look for supporting players to move to provide two passing options (girls must learn that movement off the ball and a continuous adjustment of supporting positions is essential to maintain possession)

Three-on-one teaches possession and reinforces tactical decision making.

Four-on-two possession reinforces the creation of a diamond shape to foster passing options.

- When receiving the pass, control the ball into space away from the defender, keeping the body positioned open to allow for a pass in either supporting direction

Four-on-Two Possession. This is a natural progression from three-on-one. With two defenders pressuring, both short passing options can now be covered, so the fourth player must provide a longer passing option. The shape created by the four players is that of a diamond, and they must continuously look to maintain this shape in order to keep possession of the ball.

The girl who's providing the option for the longer pass and who's positioned at the top of the diamond shape must continuously look to find the space between the two defenders.

Shielding

When a player is in limited space and is unable to pass the ball to a teammate or dribble forward, she must maintain possession by shielding the ball. Just a few seconds of shielding is enough time for a teammate to provide support for a pass or for space to be created. Space is created if the pressuring defender comes around and attempts to steal the ball.

To shield the ball, the girl must use her entire body to block the defender. By using the shoulder and arm to lean into the defender and by placing the ball at the outside of the foot farthest from the defender, the girl can create a large barrier to protect the ball.

Tactical Differences

There's little difference in the tactics between girls' soccer and boys' soccer, but the positioning of defenders away from the ball does influence the tactics taken. Girls are less able to play long passes from one side of the field to the other and from the defense to the front line, due to differences in leg strength. Instead, girls are more likely to use a combination of passes to get the ball across the field or up the field.

When defending, girls can leave attackers who are positioned farther away and can pinch in closer to the ball, without the possibility of being caught out with a long cross-field pass.

Positions

When your team has possession of the ball, every girl is an attacker; when your team doesn't have possession, every girl is a defender. Within the team, the forwards have a greater responsibility to score goals, the defenders to develop attacks and prevent the other team from scoring, and midfielders to link between the two. To create space, certain players are responsible for the left side of the field, some for the right, and some for the center.

Before playing 11-on-11 it's essential for girls to have the opportunity to play multiple positions, so that they learn and develop a good understanding of the game. To help young players get a sense of positions and to counteract their natural tendency to swarm around the ball, begin by assigning specific jobs for each girl that relate to different positions on the field:

Forwards or Attackers.
- Find an open space when the midfielders have the ball
- When you get the ball, control it and dribble toward the goal
- If you get near the goal, score by kicking the ball into the net
- When the other team's defenders have the ball, steal the ball from them
- Generally stay ahead of the midfielders

Midfielders or Halfbacks.
- Find an open space when the defenders have the ball
- If playing on the left or right, create width by moving out wide
- When you get the ball, control it and then look to pass to a forward or dribble forward
- If you can't pass to a forward or dribble, look to pass to another midfielder
- When you don't have the ball, help your defenders protect the goal
- Generally stay between the forwards and defenders

Defenders.
- Stop the other team from shooting and getting close to the goal
- Block shots and steal the ball
- When you get the ball, pass to a midfielder or forward
- When your team is attacking, move farther up the field to support the play
- Generally stay between your goal and the midfielders

Goalkeeper.
- Defend the goal and stop any shots that come toward it
- Use your hands to catch or block any balls that are in the air inside the penalty area

- Use your hands to pick up the ball if it's loose inside the penalty area
- When you have the ball in your hands, move quickly to the edge of the penalty area and roll, throw, or kick the ball to a teammate
- If the ball is outside the penalty area, use your feet to pass the ball to a teammate

Formations

When choosing a formation of players on the field, you must follow the basic necessity of having width and depth in your team, so that you can create space on the field and stretch the opposition apart. When a formation is described such as 4-4-2 or 3-3-1, it outlines the basic positions of the outfield players only and doesn't include the goalkeeper. The first number is the number of defenders, the second number is the number of midfielders, and the third number is the number of forwards.

Three-on-Three: Soccer Triangle. With three players on the team, there's no goalkeeper and there are no specific positions. Girls should try to maintain a triangular shape so that the girl with the ball always has two passing options.

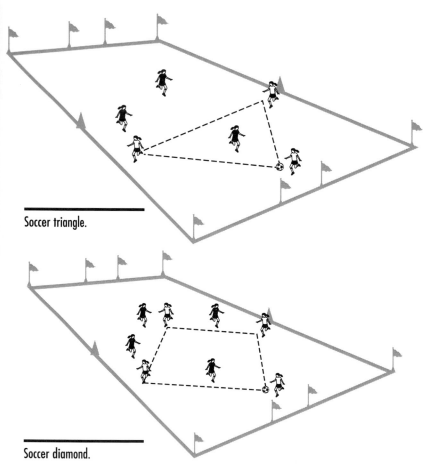

Soccer triangle.

Soccer diamond.

Four-on-Four: Soccer Diamond. With four girls on the team, players adopt a diamond formation so that the girl with the ball has a passing option on either side of her and a longer option ahead of the ball. If a goalkeeper is one of the four players, she moves up the field with the team to provide support and maintain the basic diamond shape.

Six-on-Six: 1-3-1 or 3-2. When there are six players, one will be a goalkeeper, and the remaining five will be spread over the field to create both width and depth. Your team will need two wide players, at least one forward, and at least one central defender. Where the extra player is positioned will depend on the strengths and weaknesses of the team. To provide extra support in attacking, you would use two forwards. With only five outfield players, it's important that players realize that everybody must attack and defend as a group.

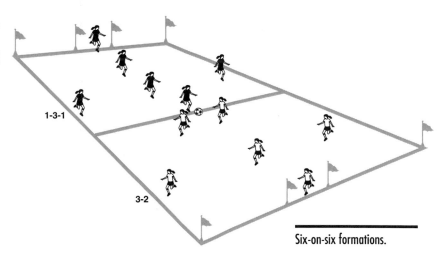

Six-on-six formations.

Eight-on-Eight. Even though an eight-on-eight game is played on a smaller-sized field than an 11-on-11 game, it's still necessary to use a formation that provides both width and depth. With seven outfield players there's a variety of formations that may be used, and you should select the one that enhances your team's strengths and minimizes your weaknesses. The formation you use will determine the style of how your team plays, so if you want to teach and develop a possession-style game, you'll need a formation with more defenders and midfielders.

4-3-0: This formation is great for teaching and developing a possession-style game. The four defenders and three midfielders allow the ball to remain in the team's control and to be played out from the back with greater success. As there's no target forward, your team must be patient and work as a unit to move the ball up the field and get players in the attacking zone. With no target player and no option to play a longer or more direct pass, it may be more difficult for your team to create goal-scoring opportunities. Similarly, with no forward, it's more difficult to put the other team's defenders under pressure in their defensive third of the field.

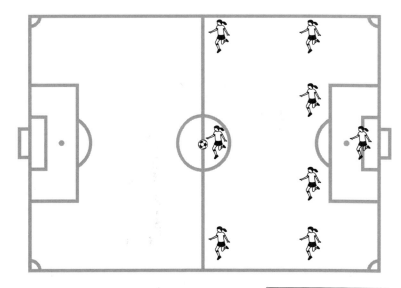

A 4-3-0 formation.

3-3-1: The 3-3-1 formation allows fewer short passing options from the goalkeeper, therefore making it more difficult to play out the ball from the back. The addition of a forward means it's easier to stretch out the opposition

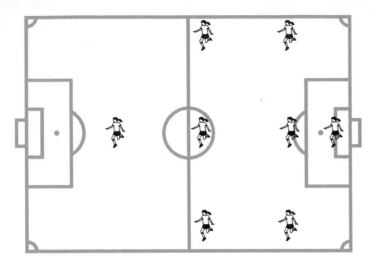

A 3-3-1 formation.

and apply greater pressure on their defenders in their defensive third of the field. It allows your team to play both a possession-style game and a more direct style of getting the ball to a target player. More attacking opportunities are created, although the one forward may at times be isolated and receive less support.

3-2-2: In this formation the addition of a second forward increases the number of attacking opportunities and provides greater support to the target player. The two forwards allow considerable pressure to be put on the opposition defense and increase the chances of winning back possession of the ball in the attacking third. With fewer midfielders and less width, however, it's more difficult to play out from the back and maintain possession of the ball, leading to a more direct style of play. The defenders and midfielders must be more proficient at playing longer-range passes, and the forwards must be able to control the ball out of the air.

11-on-11. When coaching a full-sided game, there are many different formations to choose from, with each having a variety of benefits and drawbacks. The best formation for one team may not necessarily be the best formation for your team and will often change based on the size of the field, the playing ability of the opposition, or the score of the game. Select a formation that plays to your team's strengths and minimizes your weaknesses. The following are two of the more widely used formations in girls' youth soccer.

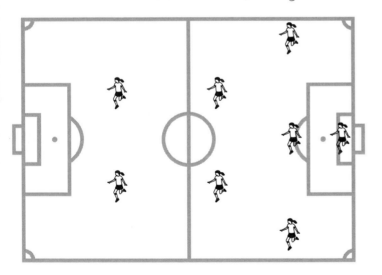

A 3-2-2 formation.

4-4-2: With four defenders, four midfielders, and two forwards, this formation is well balanced and naturally creates both width and depth in the attack. It allows for a possession-style game, with the permanent option of playing forwards who are more direct to the target. The two wide midfielders must be encouraged to join the attack; otherwise the two forwards may become isolated and have difficulty creating goal-scoring opportunities alone. It's important that these two wide midfielders have the speed, fitness level, and ability to repeatedly run up and down the field in order to beat defenders and deliver good crosses. With only two forwards it may be difficult to put the other team under pressure in their defensive third and win back possession, especially if they're playing with four defenders.

4-3-3: In this formation, the addition of a forward increases the number of players involved in the attack and may create a greater number of goal-scoring opportunities for your team. The three forwards are able to apply greater pressure on the other team's defenders, creating more opportunities to

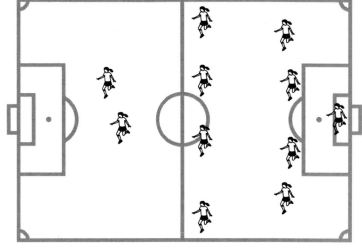

A 4-4-2 formation.

win back the ball in the attacking third of the field. The increased pressure makes it more difficult for the opposition to possess the ball and play accurate passes out from the back. But with one less midfielder it's harder for

your team to maintain possession and switch the ball, and it may leave the center of the field defensively vulnerable. In this formation it's important to have a central midfielder who's not only technically and tactically proficient but who also has the level of fitness required to meet the physical demands of the position.

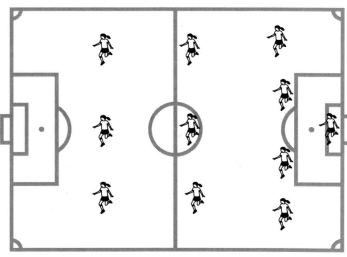

A 4-3-3 formation.

CHAPTER 10

The Practice

As a coach, you'll find that you're running practices more than anything else. You may be practicing weekly, twice a week, or even more frequently.

In order for the girls to develop and have fun in a learning environment, you must plan and structure every practice, and the practices must have a level of continuity over time. Practicing is how the players learn the game of soccer, so they must be given the opportunity to learn and develop every aspect of it. Improvement occurs through repetition and by providing the girls with progressively challenging situations from week to week.

Because there's so much to learn, and so much time and repetition are needed for techniques to become mastered and automatic, you must prioritize which techniques and tactics are most important at every stage of development. It's less important for a 6-year-old to understand positioning and more important for her to spend time developing a feel for the ball. To provide a solid foundation for your players, plan an outline of what essential techniques and tactics need to be learned and practiced now, so that they have the tools needed to master more advanced skills when they're older.

Prioritizing is vital to ensure that the girls don't miss important stages in their soccer development and that they spend sufficient time practicing and mastering the basics. For example, spending time practicing shooting with 6-year-olds is detrimental to their overall develop-

Stages of player development for soccer success.

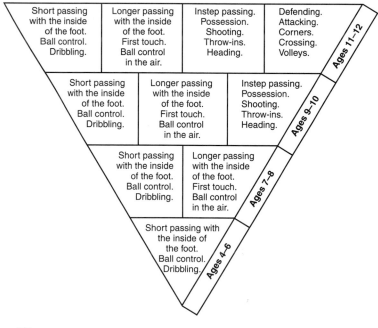

ment, as they must be given as much time as possible to become comfortable moving around with the ball at their feet. The accompanying diagram prioritizes what activities should be covered at every age group.

Practice Format

For the girls to develop a routine and to reinforce good habits, each practice must be structured and follow a similar format. If the practice is too long, players lose concentration, become bored, and no longer perceive it as being fun. The practice should last about 45 minutes with girls aged 4–6 and up to 90 minutes for ages 11–12.

The following is a template for a 90-minute practice. Prior to puberty, stretching isn't necessary, so for the entire 90 minutes each girl is given as much time with the ball as possible.

Juggling Challenge (10 minutes)

Have two different juggling challenges planned before practice starts, so that when players arrive they can go straight on the field and begin practicing. They might have 5 minutes to see how far they can juggle without dropping the ball and then 5 minutes to see how many catch juggles they can perform. Keep a note of how each girl does on each of the challenges and praise those who improve from one week to another. After several weeks set different challenges.

> To increase the amount of time spent with the ball and to maximize player development, every girl has a ball.

Starting practice as soon as the first girl gets there and allowing those who arrive early to immediately start the juggling challenge is a great way of motivating parents and players to arrive on time. Girls who arrive early get more time to spend on each challenge and are more likely to improve each week. Personal improvement that can be measured and recognition by the coach of great effort and achievement provide a high degree of satisfaction and positive reinforcement for girls.

Prior to puberty, there's no benefit for young players to warm up without the ball and to spend time stretching, so the juggling challenge is also a great way of getting players warm.

Ball Work and Dribbling (20 minutes)

For young girls to become the master of the ball and to be totally comfortable moving around with the ball at their feet under pressure and in tight spaces, as much time as possible must be spent playing fun dribbling games and learning different dribbling moves. Considerable time and repetition are needed to develop a high level of ball mastery; dribbling, ball work, and one-on-one duels should be a part of every practice with youth players.

One-on-One Duels (15 minutes)

Once basic skills have been learned and practiced through fun dribbling games, the girls must be placed in a more competitive environment to replicate the pressure that would occur in a game. This pressure comes through various one-on-one duels. Different one-on-one situations can be set up to control the level of pressure and degree of competition under which players perform. As the girls improve, the duels should then be adjusted to further increase the pressure under which moves and skills are practiced.

Technical Work (20 minutes)

As well as becoming the master of the ball, players must also learn to pass, control, head, shoot, defend, and attack. The amount of time spent on each technique over the course of the season depends on the age of the players and the number of available practice opportunities. Once again, it's important to prioritize based on age and the stage of soccer development (see the diagram on page 102). With youth players the majority of the time must be spent on passing and control, with less time spent on shooting, heading, and defending. It takes a lot of practices and many years to perfect all of these techniques, so don't expect overnight success. To maximize repetitions over a short period of time, carefully plan the games and exercises so that every girl receives as many opportunities to practice the technique as is possible. For example, if the technique is passing, setting up a game where girls work in groups of two would maximize the number of opportunities each girl has to practice passing.

With each new technique, begin by simplifying and breaking it down into smaller parts that can be practiced separately. Demonstrate each part, allowing the girls time to practice, and then demonstrate again with all the parts together. Give the girls additional time to practice, and make both individual and group corrections based on the coaching points you highlighted in your lesson plan. Monitor and record the level of progression and development so that you can continue next time from where you left off.

The younger the group of girls, the more time will be required going over and practicing the basics. Gradually over time, however, the level of complexity and pressure can be increased, so that the girls are practicing the technique in game-like situations.

Small-Sided Games (20 minutes)

Children love to play and compete against each other, so let them do just that. Divide the group into small teams and play games ranging from three-on-three to seven-on-seven. With 12 players you could have four teams of 3

With fewer players on the field during small-sided games, each girl has a greater involvement in the game and more opportunities to develop her soccer skills.

players or two teams of 6. Remember that the fewer the players on the field in each game, the greater the involvement and development of each girl. With 4- to 6-year-olds your role is to give the girls a basic understanding of the objective of soccer and then to make sure the game flows with as few stops as possible. At all times let the games flow and avoid stopping the action to correct every mistake. Encourage the girls to practice at home what they've been learning and stop the game only two or three times to make coaching points. Correct mistakes by talking to the girls individually while the game is going on.

Weekly Challenge (5 minutes)

The weekly challenge is a little bit like homework, but it's fun and gets the girls thinking about soccer throughout the week until the next practice. Demonstrate a new skill or choose a trick or a technique that you worked on earlier; challenge the girls to practice the technique and be able to perform it by the following practice. Alternatively, tell them about a soccer game that may be on TV and ask them to name five players from the teams or the goal scorers during the game—something to get them involved with soccer away from practice.

Economical Training

Soccer is a sport that involves several different components: technical, tactical, physical, and psychological. Girls must fully develop each component of the game to be able to play successfully when they're older. In order to create the most efficient learning environment and maximize development, it's crucial to plan activities and games that involve more than one component at any time. Any activities developing more than one component simultaneously are considered to be an economical form of training. For example, if you're working on a technique, use activities where players also have to make decisions so that they develop tactically as well.

In Keep-Away games (see Game 21 on page 146), players are technically developing passing and first touch, but they're also developing tactically. If you want to work on fitness, have the girls perform the activity with a ball so that they develop technically at the same time. One activity that develops all four components at the same time and that should be a part of the practice at any age is one-on-one competitions, which are a highly economical way of developing complete players.

The accompanying table highlights the importance of each component and how the role it plays in player development changes with age. The more checkmarks, the more important the role of that component in player development for a given age range.

Age	Technical	Tactical	Physical	Psychological
5–6	✓✓✓			✓✓
7–8	✓✓✓	✓		✓✓
9–10	✓✓✓	✓✓		✓✓
11–12	✓✓✓	✓✓✓	✓	✓✓
13+	✓✓✓	✓✓✓✓	✓✓	✓✓

Planning the Practice

If you have an outline of what you need to cover over the course of a season and what the priority should be at each stage of player development, you can decide how much time to dedicate to each aspect of soccer.

With a season outline you'll automatically have a topic for every practice from which you can then plan exactly what you're going to do and focus on. When you're planning each practice session, all the exercises and games can be geared toward practicing that specific topic, and all of your demonstrations and coaching points can focus on teaching and developing that topic. There will be plenty of other things to correct, but always concentrate primarily on the main topic of the session. Focusing on the topic will help you teach and coach that aspect of soccer, ahead of everything else that needs correcting.

It's vital to write down in detail what games and exercises you're going to set up and how long you want to spend on each. Make a note of what demonstrations you'll do, the mistakes you might see, and the coaching points you want to highlight. At ages where the girls are still learning to master ball-handling and dribbling moves, each session should have two topics—a dribbling topic and a technical topic.

Dribbling Topic

Each dribbling topic should be broken down into four stages:

- Warm-up
- Fundamental stage
- Game-related stage
- One-on-one stage

The *warm-up* is used to familiarize the girls with the ball once again and should involve basic dribbling at different speeds using different parts of the feet. Moves and fakes learned in previous weeks should be recapped and practiced through fun games.

In the *fundamental stage* the basics of a new move are taught and practiced. The move is simplified into small steps and then practiced slowly or stationary, with coaching corrections being made. The girls should be given many opportunities to practice the new move both standing still and while moving.

In the *game-related stage* these moves are practiced with increased pressure by having players perform while dribbling. This can be done by returning to a catcher-style game and incorporating the new move into it. Alternatively, pressure can be added by having the girls practice at a faster pace, performing the move as many times as they can in a set period of time.

The *one-on-one stage* is where the move is practiced in a competitive environment with increased and controlled pressure. The pressure can be controlled by changing the size of the playing area and by using restraining areas. If the move involves a change of direction laterally or involves going past a defender, then the one-on-one situation must be set up to replicate these actions.

Technical Topic

Each technical topic should be broken down into three stages:

- Fundamental stage
- Game-related stage
- Game-condition stage

The *fundamental stage* is the technique at its very basic. The exercises should be simple and involve practicing the technique, which is broken down into smaller steps, with limited movement and limited pressure. The exercises should provide the girls with many opportunities to practice the technique.

In the *game-related stage* the girls perform the technique with increased pressure and movement. Once again, the exercises and games should provide frequent repetition of the technique, so use small group sizes. Control the pressure by changing the size of the playing area, the number of touches, and the number of defenders involved. By performing and practicing the technique in game-like situations, but with controlled pressure, the players learn to perform the technique as they would in a real game. This is the *game-condition stage*. The game-condition stage is an actual practice scrimmage that is modified to highlight the technique being taught.

The rules of the game should be modified in order to place emphasis on the technique you're teaching. If you're working on passing, for example, you might adapt the game so that performing a set number of consecutive passes also counts as a goal, or if you're working on heading, a headed goal might be worth double. It's important to set conditions that aren't a requirement to score but that have a greater reward. This avoids situations that are unrealistic and allows players to make decisions about what to do. A condition of only being able to score a goal using the head is unrealistic, as the ball might arrive at a girl's feet 5 yards from the goal. You want her to automatically look to finish and score, whether the ball is in the air or on the ground. At the end of the practice, always remove any conditions and finish with a free-flowing game.

Organizing the Practice

Being organized is essential to providing an effective learning environment. There are several factors to help your practices become organized.

Be Punctual

Get to the practice and games early and set up the area ahead of time, so from the moment the first girl arrives it's all soccer, soccer, soccer.

If you say practice will finish at a set time, have it end then. Don't keep the girls for an extra 30 minutes, which will frustrate both players and parents. Reinforce to the parents and players the importance of arriving on time, and speak to those who repeatedly arrive late. Always start practice on time and avoid waiting for those who are late.

Be Disciplined

Have a set of rules to help you control the group and maintain the discipline during your practices. If the practices become undisciplined, they'll lose any sense of organization, and it'll be difficult to effectively teach and coach.

The rules should be simple, such as the following:

- Players should arrive on time
- Players should always bring a soccer ball to practice
- Players don't talk when the coach is talking
- On the coach's command, players have 5 seconds to be sitting down in front of the coach, ready to listen

The girls will want to get your attention, so congratulate the first two girls who are sitting down and being quiet. This demonstrates that they'll receive this positive attention if they're following the rules.

Plan for Odd Numbers

When planning each session, also make a note of how you'll change a game or exercise if you have an odd number of girls. Should someone arrive late, become injured, leave early, or fail to show up, you'll know ahead of time how to deal with the situation.

Organizational Games

If you instruct a team of 7-year-old girls to get into groups of three, you'll end up with a group of five, a group of four, girls switching groups—just utter chaos. So get players into different-size groups using fun organizational games such as the Numbers Game.

Numbers Game

Call out a number while the girls are dribbling, and have them quickly get into groups of that number. The first group to do so gets one point per player. Everybody dribbles again, and you call out a different number. The girls once again quickly form groups of that number, with the first group getting one point each. On the third or fourth occasion, call out the actual size of the group that's required for the next part of the practice, and the girls quickly get into groups of that number. If there's an odd number, the extra girl can quickly be added to a group.

Gathering Race

In order to gather the girls in quickly, so that you can demonstrate or explain a particular technique or activity, make it a race. Give them 5 seconds to be sitting down in front of you. Congratulate and praise the first two girls who are sitting and ready to listen, which will reinforce the desired result of getting the girls in quickly.

What to Avoid

In order to increase player development, every practice should avoid lines, laps, and lectures. Devote the practice time to the improvement of your players' soccer skills.

Lines. Avoid practices and exercises that involve girls waiting in lines, for when they're just watching they're not getting practice opportunities. In order to maximize repetitions and eliminate lines, have the girls work in small groups.

Laps. Avoid sending girls to run laps. Time is precious in soccer and can't be wasted if you want to develop each girl to her maximum. Running laps doesn't develop any technical aspect of soccer. To develop the physical component, dribbling and rapid changing of direction with and without the ball better replicate the demands of soccer than simply running laps.

Lectures. Avoid spending long periods of time lecturing and talking to the girls. Every moment spent talking is less time spent practicing and learning the game. The girls come to play and not to listen to the coach talk all the time, so keep corrections and coaching points brief, clear, and to the point.

Sample Practices

In the following few pages I'll lead you through a sample practice for different age groups. The practices will cover various levels of ability, from the beginner to the more advanced. These are outlines around which you can base your own practices, and they should be adjusted and tweaked to fit the particular ability level of your group. All of the games and practices are explained in greater detail in Chapters 12–15, where they're numbered consecutively. Those numbers appear next to the game for easy reference.

Ages 4–6: 45-Minute Practice

The focus of this practice is on the basics of dribbling and short passing. The fundamentals are taught in a fun-filled adventure environment. Remember that the players are 4–6-year-old girls and not teens or adults, so the more creative and animated you can become with this practice, the easier it'll be to teach them the game.

Juggling Challenge (5 minutes). As players arrive, tell them that you want to learn everyone's name, so they must spell out their name with juggles. Introducing juggling at the start will make it obvious to the parents that every girl needs a soccer ball. The juggling challenge at the start provides a way for every girl to practice at her own level as soon as she arrives.

Gathering Race. Bring the girls in quickly by giving them 5 seconds to sit down quietly in front of you. Recognize the first two players to sit down.

Ball Work and Dribbling (15 minutes). With the girls sitting down in front of you, demonstrate how to dribble the soccer ball. Highlight what part of the foot to use, how close to keep the ball to the foot, and the importance of keeping the head up. Get them to identify where their laces are on their cleats so they know what part of the foot to use when dribbling.

    Around the World (see Game 3 on page 134): Kneel down to make yourself at your players' level and briefly explain that the marked area is the ocean and the soccer ball is their boat. Grab the attention of the group by explaining the game with an expressive and animated voice. The girls are to move around the ocean, avoiding the other boats and any rocks by keeping their head up on lookout. Introduce the different countries that they're to visit one at a time and the various skills they must perform. Once all of the countries have been announced, the girls dribble around the field. On each command they move to a different side of the area and perform the required skill as quickly as possible. Randomly announce different countries for a couple of minutes.

Introduce a dribbling move: Freeze the group (see page 25) and use the Gathering Race (see page 109) to bring the girls in. Use Copy the Coach (see pages 25–26) to demonstrate and teach the dribbling move called drag back (see page 49). Because we're using a boat theme, tell players that this is a special reverse move the boats need in order to change direction. Instruct the group to explore the ocean once again but to practice changing direction with their boats by using their new move. If players are about to hit another boat, they should change direction by using the drag back. Continue to call out the different countries for them to visit.

Introduce a little pressure by adding a catcher: Freeze the group (see page 25). Announce that you're the boat police and you're going to try to stop the players from sailing their boats around the ocean. If caught, they must perform three catch juggles (see page 59) to get their boat back. The only way to avoid being caught is by doing the drag back (see page 49). After several minutes announce that you need two girls to be the new boat police. Base your selection on which girls are working the hardest to perform the drag back. These two girls then have 2 minutes to catch as many soccer balls as possible. If a player is caught or her ball leaves the playing area, she must do three drag backs before reentering the game. Move around the outside of the area and individually correct the technique of those girls who've been caught and are performing the drag back to get back into the game. Here are some common mistakes that you'll see:

- Kicking the ball backward with the heel
- Keeping the legs straight
- Not dragging the ball with the sole of the foot
- Turning to the wrong side
- Moving away slowly after the move

After 2 minutes, select two new catchers. Base this selection on which girls are working the hardest to perform the drag back using the opposite foot. Play again for 2 minutes.

Drink Break. To maximize time with the ball and reduce the amount of time lost when giving the girls a drink, make it a race. Involve the technique that you're teaching into the drink race. Freeze the group (see page 25) and use the Gathering Race (see page 109) to bring the girls in. Announce that you're going to have a race. The winners are the first three girls to do the following:

- Perform three drag backs
- Run over and take six sips of their drink
- Run back
- Perform three more drag backs
- Sit down with the ball on their head

Recognize and congratulate the first three girls to finish.

Technical Work: Short Passing with the Inside of the Foot (10 minutes).

Numbers Game: Use the Numbers Game (see Game 5 on page 135) to get the girls into groups of two. Get one girl from each group to quickly dribble her soccer ball over to the drinks area, leave it there, and run back to her partner. To simplify which girl takes the ball, say that the smallest or tallest in each group does so.

Monsters, Inc. II: Bring the girls in to you and demonstrate the technique used to pass the ball with the inside of the foot. Highlight how to aim with the nonkicking foot, how to keep the ankle of the passing foot firm, and what surface of the foot to use. Get the girls to tap the inside of the foot so they know what surface to use. If they have difficulty keeping the passing foot firm, give them an imaginary key so that they can lock their ankle in the correct position. Introduce the game Monsters, Inc. II (see Game 13 on pages 140–41). As the girls are passing, move around the group, observing, identifying, and correcting individual problems. With this age group it's often necessary to physically move limbs so that they're positioned correctly. Here are some common mistakes that you'll see:

- The nonkicking foot pointing away from the target
- The inside of the kicking foot not facing the target
- Loose and floppy ankles
- Contact being made with the side of the ball
- Follow-through away from the direction of the target
- Legs crossing over

After the first game, play a second game with the girls using the opposite foot.

Stuck in the Mud: Once the girls have performed the short pass while stationary, it's time to practice the technique while moving. Before starting the game, use the Gathering Race to bring the girls in. Demonstrate the technique that should be used to pass the ball through the legs. Once again, highlight how to aim with the nonkicking foot, how to keep the ankle of the passing foot firm, and what surface of the foot to use. Play Stuck in the Mud (see Game 14 on page 141) and take on the role of the mud monster. After 2 minutes have two girls be the mud monsters so you can observe the girls and can identify and correct individual problems.

Small-Sided Game (10 minutes). Three-on-Three: It's important to finish by letting the girls practice what they've just learned in a game. Use the Numbers Game (see Game 5 on page 135) to get the girls into groups of three. Play three-on-three with small goals and no boundaries. Try to keep the game flowing with few stoppages. For the first few practices with this age group, you'll need to reinforce the objective of getting the ball in the other team's goal. During the game give encouragement to those girls who pass and control the ball and point out any good passing technique to the whole group.

Weekly Challenge. At the end of the practice, bring the girls in and tell them how well they did. If there are parents around, bring them in also. Get the parents to give the girls a round of applause for doing so well. In order to keep the players practicing over the week, send them home with a weekly challenge. Challenge each girl to be able to complete five drag backs with the right foot and five drag backs with the left foot as fast as possible. Remember to ask them about this task and challenge them to perform at the following practice.

If you have any announcements for the parents or need to remind them about anything, such as bringing a ball to practice or being punctual, this is the time to do it. Finish with a team cheer and tell the girls that you look forward to seeing them all next time.

Ages 7–8: 60-Minute Practice

The focus of this practice is on dribbling moves to beat defenders and on basic first touch and passing. The fundamentals are taught through fun games rather than exercises and drills. Although less emphasis is placed on using a story or adventure theme in this practice, it's still important to be imaginative and animated with 7- and 8-year-olds.

Juggling Challenge (5 minutes). Total Body Juggling: Record how many juggles each girl achieves (see Game 28 on page 149) and praise those who improved from the previous week.

Gathering Race. Bring the girls in quickly by giving them 5 seconds to be sitting down in front of you. Recognize the first two players to sit down.

Ball Work and Dribbling (10 minutes). Kneel down at the girls' level and briefly explain that they must keep their soccer ball in the area at all times. If it goes out, they must do 10 juggles to reenter the area. While they're dribbling, move around and kick several soccer balls out of the area as the girls try to dribble away from you.

Introduce a dribbling move: Freeze the group while the players are dribbling and play Copy the Coach (see pages 25–26) to demonstrate and teach a dribbling move called the scissors move (see pages 53–54). Break the move down into stages and highlight the following movements:

- Position the body behind and to the left side of the ball
- Move the right leg and shoulder across the ball
- Shift and lower the body
- Use the outside of the left foot to move away with the ball
- Accelerate into space

Kick Out: Select two girls and give them 1 minute to kick out as many soccer balls as possible in a game of Kick Out (see Game 4 on pages 134–35). Select the two girls working the hardest to practice the scissors. To reenter the game if the ball goes out, a girl must complete the scissors five times. While the girls are playing, move around and individually correct the technique of any girls outside the area. Here are some common mistakes that you'll see:

- Moving only the leg over the ball
- No movement of the body across the ball
- Keeping the legs straight
- No change in the direction of the ball following the move
- No change in speed

One-on-one competitions are a great way to develop the technical, tactical, physical, and psychological components of soccer all at the same time.

Play several rounds of Kick Out, selecting two different girls each time. Select those girls who are working the hardest to perform the scissors with the opposite foot and then using alternate feet. After the final round, use the Numbers Game to get the girls organized into groups of two. Use the Gathering Race to get the girls sitting down in front of you quickly.

One-on-One (10 minutes). One-on-One to a Line: Select one girl who was performing the scissors well to help you demonstrate One-on-One to a Line (see Game 12 on page 140). Highlight the importance of having confidence when taking on defenders and the importance of changing direction and changing speed. Encourage the use of the scissors move by giving two points to anybody who scores a goal after completing the move. Give the group 5 seconds to get in position with their partners and be ready to play. Then, on your command, they can begin. Play for 3 minutes and then move around one girl in every pair so that all girls play somebody different in the next game. If you need to make any coaching points or demonstrate again, quickly bring the group in to you to do so. While the girls are playing, move around and make any individual corrections.

Drink Break. Freeze the group (see page 25) and use the Gathering Race (see page 109) to bring the girls in. Announce that you're going to have a race. The winners are the first three girls to do the following:

- Perform the scissors move five times with the right leg
- Run over and take six sips of their drink
- Run back
- Perform the scissors move five times with the left leg
- Sit down with the ball on their head

Recognize and congratulate the first three girls to finish.

Technical Work: Passing and First Touch (15 minutes). Numbers Game: Use the Numbers Game (see Game 5 on page 135) to get the girls into groups of two with one ball.

Soccer Mall: Working in groups of two players, the girls move around, passing the ball between a series of gates in Soccer Mall (see Game 17 on pages 143–44). If they miss a gate or if the ball stops moving, they must start again. After they've made several practice runs with the left foot and the right foot, restrict the number of touches they may take between each gate to place greater emphasis on the first touch. Here are some common mistakes that you'll see:

- The inside or outside of the kicking foot not facing the gate
- Loose and floppy ankles
- Follow-through away from the direction of the gate
- First touch that's too soft, so the ball gets stuck underneath the feet
- First touch that's too hard, so the ball runs away out of control
- First touch that's going behind the player because she hasn't positioned her body to control the ball

First-Touch Races (see Game 35 on page 151): Observe, identify, and correct individual problems.

Small-Sided Game (15 minutes). Four-on-Four: Play four-on-four with small goals and no boundaries. Try to keep the game flowing with few stoppages. Allow goals to be scored by either getting the ball across the goal line or by making four consecutive passes. Continually emphasize that every time a girl receives the ball, she should play a pass to herself with her first touch. Point out good control and passing technique to the whole group.

Weekly Challenge. At the end of the practice bring the girls in and tell them how well they did. Get them to give each other a round of applause for working so hard. Challenge each girl to be able to complete five scissors with the right foot and five scissors with the left foot as fast as possible for the next practice. In addition, demonstrate one way to get the ball off the ground without using the hands and ask the players to come up with another way for the next practice.

Be sure to challenge the girls about this at the following practice. Give any announcements or reminders to the parents, such as bringing a ball to practice and being punctual for practices and games. Then finish with a team cheer.

Ages 9–10: 90-Minute Practice

The focus of this practice is on developing advanced dribbling moves and learning the roles of the first and second defender in small-group exercises and in the game. More emphasis is placed on creating a competitive environment, with girls competing against each other in exercises and small-sided games rather than in animated adventure games.

Juggling Challenge (5 minutes). Feet-Only Juggling (see Game 29 on page 149): Record how many juggles each girl achieves and congratulate those who've improved from the previous week.

Ball Work and Dribbling (15 minutes). Knock Out Five (see Game 10 on page 139): If a girl has her ball knocked out of the area, she must perform five roll flicks and five stop turns before coming back in.

Introduce a dribbling move: Freeze the girls (see page 25) while they're all dribbling and quickly sit them down so that you can demonstrate and teach a new dribbling move called the squeeze push (see page 54). Break the move down into stages and highlight the following movements:

1. Dribble with the ball out in front and slightly to the right of the body
2. Roll the right foot over the ball so that it moves across the body from right to left
3. Squeeze and push the ball with the outside of the right foot back away to the right
4. Accelerate into the space

Here are some common mistakes that you'll see:

- Rolling the foot over the ball and allowing the legs to cross
- Keeping the legs straight and losing balance

- Standing on the ball
- No change in direction or speed following the move

One-on-One (15 minutes). Diagonal One-on-One (see Game 11 on page 139): Each girl plays four games against different opponents, with each game lasting 3 minutes. If you need to make any coaching points or demonstrate again, quickly bring the group in to you to do so. While they're playing, move around and make any individual corrections.

Drink Break/Heading Challenge. After the final game, bring the girls in and congratulate those who did well. Challenge the girls to quickly get a drink and then with a partner complete as many consecutive headers back and forth as possible. While they're practicing their heading, set up the area for the next exercises.

Technical/Tactical Work (25 minutes). Two-on-Two to a Line: Set up two or three areas to play Two-on-Two to a Line (see Game 81 on page 181). If you have extra players, set up a side game of One-on-One to a Line (see Game 12 on page 140). Select three girls to help you with the demonstration. Explain the role of the first defender and the importance of delaying the attack and being patient. Highlight the position of the second defender at a distance and angle close enough to cover the first defender if she should be beaten but also close enough to pressure the immediate attacker if the ball is passed. While the girls are playing, explain the positioning of the second defender. After 6 minutes of play, bring the group in and demonstrate how the position changes when the attacker dribbles the ball diagonally across the playing area. Review the role of the first defender to stay with the attacker as she dribbles across the area and the importance of communication. Rotate the teams around so that they have different com-petition and play the next game. While they're playing, move around and make any individual corrections. Play a total of three or four games all together.

Small-Sided Game (20 minutes). Six-on-Six: Play six-on-six with goalkeepers. Try to keep the game flowing with few stoppages. As possession is lost or as the opposition passes the ball from one side of the field to the other, indicate which girl is the first defender and which one is the second defender. Where appropriate, stop the game to highlight good positioning by the first and second defenders.

Weekly Challenge. At the end of the practice, bring the girls in and tell them how well they did. Challenge each girl to be able to complete the squeeze push five times with the right foot and five times with the left foot as fast as possible for the next practice. Be sure to challenge them on this at the following practice. In addition, select a game that's on television and ask the girls to watch it, looking to see if they can recognize the first and second defenders every time the ball is passed. Give any announcements or reminders to the parents, such as bringing a ball to practice and being punctual. Then finish with a team cheer.

Questions and Answers

Q. When I gather the players in to demonstrate a technique, I always have a few girls who immediately start talking and soon distract the others. What should I do?

A. At the very first practice you must let them know the team rules and remind them whenever necessary.

Rule 1: Never talk when the coach is talking
Rule 2: Always listen when the coach is talking

If a girl isn't paying attention, you can focus on her by asking her a question regarding what you've just said. She'll obviously not know the answer because she was talking. Congratulate the girl who does answer the question correctly and indicate that the first player didn't know the answer because she was talking. With girls who are repeatedly losing focus and talking, position them away from each other and at the front of the group when demonstrating. When demonstrating or making a coaching point, remember to keep it brief. Children have a shorter attention span, so talking too long may lead to a loss of focus and to chatting among players.

Q. One of the girls comes to practice solely to hang out and socialize. She shows no interest in practicing hard and is continuously fooling around, leading some of her friends to do the same thing. How can I get her to work harder and stop disrupting the practice?

A. Begin by stating how important her friends are to her and by mentioning that her teammates are very keen to learn and improve their soccer ability. Explain that when she's fooling around, she's limiting not only her development as a soccer player but also her friends' development. At the end of practice, speak to her parents about her behavior and how it's disrupting the rest of the team. If the behavior continues, have the girl sit out and watch the other girls. Let her know that when she's ready to practice like the rest of the team and help her friends, she can go back in. If she's still disrupting the learning environment at the end of the season, you may consider speaking to her parents or your club administrator about moving her to a different team. Remember the needs of the many outweigh the needs of the few.

Q. I have three girls on my under-10 team that are extremely talented and much better than the other players. The parents approached me because they're concerned that what I'm teaching is too basic for their daughters. What should I do to challenge these girls?

A. When working in pairs or groups, match the three girls up so that they're together and compete against each other. This will force them to perform and practice under greater pressure. If you're coaching a basic technique that they may have already mastered, insist they practice with their weaker foot. Give them individual challenges, such as seeing how many step overs they can perform in 1 minute, or move them into competitive situations sooner. At the end of the session give them a preview of a technique or move that's more advanced, so that they can practice between sessions.

Q. How long should my practices be?

A. The length of the practices should be determined by the age of the group. A 5-year-old has a shorter attention span than a 12-year-old, so the younger girls' practices should be shorter. Practices for 4- to 6-year-olds should last approximately 45 minutes, while 7- to 9-year-olds should practice for 60 minutes. Practices for girls older than 10 should be no more than 90 minutes long.

Q. I have a group of 5- and 6-year-old beginners. This is my second season with them, and although the girls are having a lot of fun, I don't see any improvement from last season. Should I move on and introduce new dribbling games and moves, or should I continue going over the ones from last season?

A. At this age, creating an environment where the girls are comfortable and having fun is the most important thing. As it takes a long period of time for the basics to be mastered, keep going over and practicing what you've taught them so far. For those girls that pick up techniques quicker, encourage them to practice moves with their weaker foot.

Q. My 12-year-old girls just want to play and scrimmage all the time at practice. Is this a bad thing?

A. It's often said that the game is the greatest teacher. Without instruction and correction, however, players will only repeat and practice poor technique. So, no, it's not a bad thing if, while they're playing, you can correct both individual technique and group tactics. Playing small scrimmages of three-on-three or four-on-four will increase player involvement in these games and improve their development. If the girls still need to learn and master basic techniques, then you'll still need to incorporate skill work in the practice. Keep the players interested by making any technical exercises competitive and team oriented.

Coaching the Game

The game is where the girls put to the test all they've learned and compete against another team. More often than not, one team will win and the other will lose. Occasionally the game will end in a tie. In many individual sports, such as running or swimming, if you're faster than all the other competitors, then you'll win. In soccer, however, this isn't the case. As a team you can be faster, stronger, and technically and tactically better than the opposition, and you can totally outplay and outshoot them, but you still might not win.

In soccer it's not the best team that necessarily wins, but rather the team that scores the most goals.

With this in mind, it's important not to judge your team's ability and success solely on the result of the game. Instead, achieve satisfaction and measure success based on how the team competes and performs.

Preparing for the Game

Remember the 5 Ps: Proper Preparation Prevents Poor Performance. Preparing for each game initially involves making sure all the players and parents know where to go, what time to be there, what to bring, and what to wear. At the last practice before the game, give out directions to the field along with information on what time they need to meet, what color uniform they need to wear, and what they need to bring, such as a ball, uniform, shin guards, cleats, and drink. If this is a first game for players and parents, send this information out again by e-mail the day before the game.

Arriving 5 minutes before kickoff isn't good preparation, so give your players plenty of time to get ready. With teams up to the age of 9, have the girls arrive at least 30 minutes before the kickoff, and with 10- to13-year-olds, have them be at the field at least 45 minutes before the game. If parents are going to be late or find themselves stuck in traffic, get them into the habit of calling you on your cell phone as early as possible.

If you're playing at home and your team is responsible for club duties, such as putting the goals up or the flags out, delegate which parents are assigned to helping you for each game. They'll need to meet you earlier than the rest of the team. In addition, set up a schedule ahead of time designating which parents are responsible for any team snacks, such as oranges at half-time. If player passes (sometimes known as player cards) are checked by the referee before each game, be sure you keep them in a safe place and bring them with you to each game.

On the actual day of the game, arrive earlier than the players so that you can assess the field location and select a good meeting place and warm-up area. On hot sunny days find a shaded area close to where you'll warm up, and use this as the meeting place. When the girls arrive, direct them to the meeting place and give them a few minutes to relax and socialize before beginning the warm-up. Plan beforehand what will be involved in the warm-up and whether you or an assistant will get the girls warmed up.

Game Day Warm-Up

A warm-up is required to prepare the girls physically and mentally for the game. It prepares the team to play beginning with the first whistle and to avoid starting the game slowly. The length of the warm-up and the different activities used will change with the age of the team. From the ages of 4 to 12 it's essential that you always provide an environment where you give the girls as much time with the ball as possible, so the warm-up should be done with the ball. A warm-up without the ball and stretching have no beneficial effect and are not a necessity for players in this age range. Jogging, movement without the ball, and stretching should not be introduced until around the age of puberty.

The warm-up should generally involve three stages, all done at an intensity that's sufficient to increase the heart rate yet light enough not to wear the girls out. With 4- to 6-year-olds only the first two stages are needed, and with older players an additional fourth stage may be added that involves the skills specific to different positions.

Individual Stage

The individual stage should be used to increase the girls' heart rate and familiarize them with dribbling and ball control. Use activities and games where the girls need to move around with the ball, change direction at speed, and practice moves and juggling. The goalkeeper should be incorporated into the warm-up by having her move around bouncing and catching the ball, alternating throwing the ball up in the air to catch it and rolling it along the ground to dive for it.

Group Stage

The group stage should be used to prepare the girls for passing, first touch, possession, and shooting. Use different passing activities for pairs of players or set up small groups of keep-away. While two groups are playing keep-away, work with a small group on shooting. Be sure to rotate the groups so that they all get a chance to shoot on goal. Avoid lining the team up to shoot one at a time, as this doesn't provide enough practice opportunities to be used in a warm-up.

Team Stage

The final stage of the warm-up is the team stage, which is used to get the girls to play at game speed and make game decisions. Create two teams and use a numbers-up situation (i.e., the team with possession has more players) to keep possession of the ball. This possession could involve switching the ball to small goals or incorporate the goalkeeper for attacking possession.

Each stage of the warm-up should last about the same length of time (approximately 6–8 minutes), with a smooth transition from one to the other. It should become a routine and involve activities and exercises the girls are comfortable doing. Try a variety of activities the girls have done before, and eventually determine through trial and error which activities work best for your team.

Team Talk

Depending on the duration of the warm-up, bring the girls in approximately 10 minutes before the kickoff so that you can talk to them in greater detail about the game. The girls will already be excited and self-motivated to play, so this time is best spent instructing rather than motivating. If you sense they're nervous about the game, build their confidence by indicating how well you think they can play. Reinforce playing well and having fun, rather than the result of the game. Never create unwanted pressure by stressing how important winning the game is. Instruct your players about how you want the team to play and set some small achievable performance-oriented goals for the first half. Measurable goals such as making a set number of consecutive passes, taking a set number of shots, winning a set number of headers, or switching the ball a set number of times can all be used to emphasize how you want the team to play.

Announce who's playing in what position and the role of each position. Highlight the importance of each individual performance and how it affects the overall performance of the team. If necessary, you can talk about

Coaching Advice

"The younger the team, the more important it is to place emphasis on achieving performance-oriented goals such as completing passes or creating shots on goal, with less emphasis placed on the score of the game."

the opposition and what your players might do to counteract how the other team plays. After the team talk and before the players go out on the field to start the game, bring them in for some final words of encouragement and a team cheer.

Game Etiquette

Officials

Good sportsmanship—treating the other team, the officials, and other players with respect—begins with the example set by the coach. If you scream and yell at referees, the parents and then the players will believe this is an acceptable way to behave. You must explain to both the players and their parents that the referee will make some wrong calls or calls with which they might disagree, but the referee's decision is final. No degree of screaming or shouting will get the referee to change a decision. They must understand that the referee has to make difficult decisions in a split second, and they must respect the decision that's made.

Teammates

The girls must always respect and appreciate their teammates, no matter what each girl's ability, and they must never criticize or point blame. If a girl makes a mistake, her teammates should support and encourage her so that she can regain confidence for the rest of the game. Once again, the example must come from the coach. If you hear a girl criticize a teammate, it's important to deal with the situation immediately and let her know that such comments aren't allowed. Explain to her why it's an unacceptable way to treat a teammate and how she should instead give encouragement and support. If you have to take a girl off the field during a game for criticizing another player, then do so; she'll learn immediately not to do it again. As you set the standard, it's vital that you never verbally criticize any player, no matter how serious an error she makes. If a girl makes a bad mistake, she knows about it already. The last thing she needs is for the coach to tell her about it. The coach should make corrections but never criticize. If a particularly egregious error has been made, wait a few minutes or after the game to discuss it to allow the player to focus and understand exactly what should have been done.

The Opposition

The opposition is not the enemy; they are children playing a game. You should teach your girls to play tough and aggressively, but they should never be dirty players and should always show respect for the other team, whether you win or lose. Your team should be gracious in victory and defeat and should line up at the end of the game to shake hands with the opposition

Coaching Advice

"If a girl makes a mistake, keep her in the game and give her encouragement so that she's forced to keep playing and has no time to dwell on the error. If you take her out, she may just sit and think about her mistake, over and over in her head. She may feel she's let the team down and then be petrified of making a mistake the next time she's on the field."

Teams should line up at the end of the game and thank the opposition.

and to thank them for the game. If the other team doesn't display the same sportsmanship toward your team, don't lower your standards. Always teach your girls to play with dignity, and never allow them to react or mouth off, no matter how much they're provoked. Teams and individuals lacking in sportsmanship will often become more frustrated when the team they're playing against shows no reaction and just continues to play the game.

If a girl does play dirty, mouths off, or gets involved in an incident, deal with the situation as soon as you can. If she's on the field, take her off, sit her down, and explain to her why her behavior isn't acceptable. If the situation is serious, keep her out for the whole game to reinforce that her actions won't be tolerated.

Girls who are naturally quick-tempered usually haven't had sufficient experience to learn how to deal with their temper and so may retaliate if provoked. If a girl is kicked and reacts by kicking back, explain to her that you understand why she did it, but that it's still not an acceptable way to react. Explain to the other girls what can be learned from individual situations like this and stress the importance of abiding by the rules and playing with dignity.

The Four-Goal Rule

With young children it's important to always consider the consequences of running up the score on the opposition. Running up the score is a demoralizing and soul-destroying experience for the children on the losing team and provides little developmental benefit to those on the winning team. If you have a comfortable lead of four or more goals, avoid running up the score by playing girls in different positions and giving them a range of challenges. Allow them to attempt to score only from a header, after they've made a set number of passes, or after everybody on the team has passed the ball.

Coaching the First Half

During the first half, observe your team as a whole. Avoid just following the play and instead get into the habit of focusing on positioning and movement off the ball. If the defenders have the ball, look at how the forwards are moving. If the left midfielder is the immediate defender, look at where the right midfielder and right defender are positioned. The older the team and the more competitive the environment, the greater the need may be to observe how the opposition is playing. Spending the first few minutes of the game watching the other team will allow you to determine what formation they're using and whether they're trying to play a possession style or a more direct style of play. While observing the game, reinforce to your players what you've done in practice and be positive throughout. If a girl just keeps kicking the ball when it comes to her, encourage her to control it first and then pass it. Young players have a limited tactical understanding of the game, so any instruction must be specific. If you want a 7-year-old to move up the field, be specific and tell her how far to move up.

Although it's important to give instruction, don't overcoach. If you continuously talk and give information during games, your key coaching points will just get lost among everything else you're saying. To avoid falling into the trap of overcoaching, just occasionally give instruction and re-inforcement; instead, write down any individual and team coaching points. Whenever a girl is substituted, spend a minute with her to go over what she did well and to make any individual corrections that you identified. Never criticize, and always be positive in your comments.

Halftime

As there are no time-outs in soccer, the halftime period is the only opportunity you have to talk to your team, make any corrections, and prepare them for the second half. When the girls come off the field, give them enough time to get a drink, sit down, and have a small snack. The halftime drink should be either water or a sports drink, not soda, and the small halftime snack to help replenish energy should be a piece of fruit.

Go over the notes you wrote down from the first half

A piece of fruit at halftime is a great way to replenish energy.

and identify no more than three points that you want to highlight to the team. If you give the players too much information at halftime, very little of what you say will be absorbed, so keep it simple and brief. Always mention at least one positive point and recognize any individuals who are playing particularly well. Calling the team's attention to any good performance not only reinforces good performance by the team but also builds player confidence and self-esteem.

After your three coaching points, set new performance-oriented goals for the second half. Announce who will start in what position and finish with some important words of motivation and encouragement. Before the players go out onto the field, lead them in a team cheer.

Playing Time and Substitutions

Before the start of the season, determine your general philosophy on playing time. At the first team meeting or before the first game of the season, announce your philosophy to all the parents and players. Often with young players the club or league will have rules regarding playing time, such as every girl should have equal time or every girl should play at least half a game. In these situations it's important to have a balanced team throughout the game. Having all your strongest players on the field at once may weaken the team when substitutions are made, so stagger who is out at what times and keep the team balanced. You'll need to make a substitution plan before each game so that you know which girl goes on at what time and in which position.

Even if your club or league doesn't have a mandatory rule regarding playing time, you should follow a similar policy. Up to the age of 12 it's vital that every girl plays equal time or at least half a game. The fewer opportunities girls get to play in games and execute what they've learned in practice, the less likely they are to develop. If a girl with less ability only gets one-quarter of the playing time, then she'll fall even further behind. In addition to providing young players with as much playing time as possible, it's also important to give them playing time at a variety of positions.

Your policy on playing time should vary based on the age and ability of the team and also on any other rules you have regarding attendance at practice and punctuality. For example, players may be guaranteed equal playing time only if they attend practice and arrive on time for the game. If they miss a practice or are late to the game, then playing time is reduced. A well-managed policy on playing time is a great way of controlling attendance at practices and punctuality. As players move into their teens and into high school, playing time must also begin to reflect individual effort and performance. If every girl attends practice and arrives on time, those who are performing well in the game and giving the greatest effort should be rewarded with more playing time.

A Substitution Plan

In order to keep your team balanced and to provide every girl with as much playing time as possible, you need a substitution plan outlining who replaces each starting player and at what time. Although girls will get injured or need to come out at unexpected times, it's simplest to keep as close to this initial plan as possible. If you have a club policy where every girl plays equal time, begin by figuring out how many minutes each girl should play.

For example, say there are 13 girls on the team. The game is nine-on-nine and lasts 50 minutes. There are two girls each game who spend a period as the goalkeeper.

Playing Time = (# of players on field ÷ # of girls on team) x duration of game

Playing Time = (9 ÷ 13) x 50 minutes ≈ 34 minutes

Every girl should therefore play approximately 34 minutes, or 17 minutes per half. You could substitute every 17 minutes, every 8½ minutes, or every 4½ minutes.

When to Substitute. Because players coming onto the field take a few minutes to get used to the pace and tempo of the game and because you want the game to flow as much as possible, avoid substituting players in and out every 2–3 minutes. Give the girls at least 7–12 minutes of playing time before substituting other players.

In this plan, the simplest and most effective time to make changes is to substitute all four players every 8½ minutes.

Period of Game	Players Out
0–8½ min.	10, 11, 12, 13
8½–17 min.	6, 7, 8, 9
17–25 min.	2, 3, 4, 5
Halftime	
25–33½ min.	1, 13, 12, 11
33½–42 min.	7, 8, 9, 10
42–50 min.	3, 4, 5, 6

The girls numbered 1 and 2 both have more playing time because they are the two goalkeepers. Player 1 is in goal for the entire first half, and player 2 is in goal for the entire second half. Each girl also gets some playing time out of the goal.

Before each girl enters the game, tell her where she's going to play and who she's replacing. Have her watch the player she's replacing for 2 minutes, and then explain to her how you want her to play that position. After the substitution has been made, follow the player for about 30 seconds just to make sure she's gone into the correct position. Sometimes you may tell a girl to play left midfield, but she only hears the midfield part and ends up playing out of position. Observe each girl's positioning immediately after she enters the game, and reposition her if any temporary lapses in concentration have caused her to be in the wrong place.

When a girl is substituted out of the game and comes off the field, get her to take a quick drink before you talk to her about what she did well and what areas need improvement. No matter how poorly a girl is playing, it's important to be positive about what her strengths are and what she should do when she reenters the game.

Postgame Talk

After the game, get your team into a routine whether they've played well or poorly, whether they've won or lost. They should immediately jog in and line up to shake hands with the other team and the referee, thanking them for the game. Girls aged 12 and older should have a short jog and stretch to cool down before gathering for the postgame talk.

In order to reinforce the importance of measuring success based on player performance and development, rather than game results, also bring the parents in for the postgame talk. If you're highly emotional after a game, take a few minutes to compose yourself before talking to the group.

Your postgame talk should be based primarily on the team's performance and effort, rather than the result of the game. Let the girls know when you're happy with the way the way they played and when you're disappointed. Always find something positive from the game to praise, and also highlight things that need improvement. If there are one or two girls who've played an excellent game, let the others know how well they played.

Sometimes you'll need to put aside your personal disappointment at a game's result and boost your team's morale by letting them know how pleased you are with their effort and performance. When your team has played well but hasn't won, ask the girls how they thought they played. This will help them learn to understand that a good performance isn't necessarily result oriented. On other occasions you may need to let the players know that although they won the game, they didn't perform as well as they could and that you're disappointed with the way they played. When talking about the game, avoid directly blaming individuals for mistakes and instead speak about what corrections need to be made in order to improve. At the end of your postgame talk, always finish with a positive comment. Remember the Feedback Sandwich (see page 19).

Sometimes after a particularly poor performance the less said the better. Saying very few words will let the girls know that you're unhappy with their effort and performance. Instead, speak to them in more depth at the next practice.

Coaching Advice

"When you line up to thank the opposing team, give their players some words of encouragement and make a point of giving special attention to anybody who played particularly well. Those girls will remember and be thankful for your words of praise, especially if they've lost the game."

Questions and Answers

Q. I have four girls on my under-12 team who are exceptional and at a higher level than most of the other players. They're becoming frustrated in games when somebody isn't playing well, and they've even begun criticizing some of the other girls. How should I deal with this issue?

A. If you see signs of frustration or tension between players, immediately talk to the girls involved. Explain to them that every player develops at a different rate. The best players at 12 years old may not be the best at 17 years old. Stress to them that in any team setting there's a variety of levels of play, and that they must use their own ability to help improve their teammates' performance, so that as a whole the team gets better. If the overall team gets better, they'll get better. As they are currently the more advanced players, it's up to them to help their teammates improve. Let them know that criticism doesn't improve or help their teammates, so they should instead give encouragement and help build confidence if a mistake is made.

Q. What should the girls drink at halftime—a sports drink or water?

A. Sports drinks provide fluid as well as sugar for energy and electrolytes to replace those that are lost in sweat. However, sometimes sports drinks are too high in sugar and can cause cramps or nausea. With young girls, who are less likely to sweat heavily, water is usually the best choice.

Q. I have two players who regularly arrive at practices and games 10–15 minutes late. I know it's not the girls' fault, because their parents drive them, but it's very disrupting to the flow of practices. What should I do to address this issue?

A. Even though it's not necessarily the players' fault, if considerable emphasis is placed on punctuality they'll do a great job of pestering their parents to get them there on time. Always start the practice on time and begin with fun measurable activities such as juggling challenges. At the end of practice congratulate those who improved at these activities. Those who arrived late and never had a chance to participate in these challenges will be unable to tell you they've improved. This lack of participation and inclusion should lead to a greater desire to be there on time at the next practice. Explain to the parents that their daughter is missing out on these activities by arriving late and that her soccer development is being limited. Explain to the parents that their daughter's playing time will be affected if she continues to be late to practices and games. Once you've set up a system where playing time is affected by punctuality, you must be prepared to enforce it, even if it means you sometimes play with a weakened team.

Coaching Advice

"Always remind the parents how important it is just to encourage and support their daughters from the sideline, rather than trying to coach and give instruction. Parental instruction that's different from that of the coach leads to player confusion; if the advice is incorrect, it can result in poor technique or tactics."

PART TWO

Exercises and Games: Foundations for the Growth of Players and Coaches

CHAPTER 12

Dribbling, Passing, Juggling, and Ball Control

Dribbling

Monsters, Inc. 1

Purpose: To develop dribbling skills and movement with the ball	**Equipment:** 1 ball per girl
	Time: 10 to 15 minutes
Number of Players: Any	**Ages:** 4 to 6

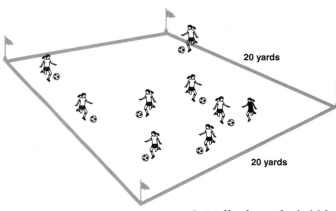

20 yards

20 yards

← dribble with the ball
← run without the ball
← pass the ball
flag
cone
ball

This adventure game is based on a popular animated movie. Create an area 20 yards by 20 yards. This is the town of Monstropolis. The girls on your team work for a company called Monsters, Incorporated, the largest scary factory on the planet. Screams are collected and refined into clean energy, which is needed to power the city of Monstropolis. The girls who collect the most scream points become the characters Sulley and Mike Wazowski, who are the top-rated scarers at the company.

Initially the girls dribble around the established area and collect screams. Whenever factory CEO Henry J. Waternoose (the coach) shouts "Freeze," the girls must place one foot on the soccer ball and scream for 3 seconds. The girl in the most space gets one scream point.

Explain to the girls that they can use three speeds to explore Monstropolis. Speed 1 is slow, like Roz, a slug-like character from the movie. Speed 2 is fast, like Sulley, and speed 3 is super fast, like Mike Wazowski. When you shout a number or a character, players must dribble at that speed. If their soccer ball hits another soccer ball or if it leaves the area, they must perform three catch juggles (see page 59), saying "Sorry, Mr. Waternoose."

Eventually Mr. Waternoose becomes disgruntled with all of the girls and wants to prevent them from exploring the city. If you can place your foot on a soccer ball, that girl must leave the area and perform three catch juggles before coming back in. Try to catch all the girls.

Introduce a secret called laughter and demonstrate a move to be associated with it, such as the drag back. If the girls can perform the move while laughing, then you're frozen with shock for 3 seconds, allowing them enough time to run away into a new space. Anybody who avoids capture gains five scream points. After a period of time allow two girls to play Mr. Waternoose. Select the two girls who are working the hardest on their dribbling.

Body Parts 2

Purpose: To develop dribbling skills and confidence while controlling a ball in a confined area	**Equipment:** 1 ball per girl
	Time: 5 to 10 minutes
	Ages: 4 to 6
Number of Players: Any	

Create an area 20 yards by 20 yards as your adventure world. Each girl dribbles around and explores adventure world. If her soccer ball leaves the area or collides with another, then she must spell her name with catch juggles (see page 59). This creates an understanding of finding space while trying to stay in an area.

While the players are dribbling around, shout out a body part. The girls must very quickly place that part of their body on the ball. They're not allowed to use their hands, so they must use their foot to initially stop the ball. This creates a situation where they must attempt to dribble with their heads up and keep the ball close to them. Be imaginative and call out entertaining body parts, such as the ear or eyebrow!

Once the girls have grasped the idea of the game, give them a minute to explore adventure world. After every four touches they must place a different part of their body on the ball. Challenge the girls to see how many different parts of their body they can use.

Progression. While the girls are dribbling, call out either "Heads" or "Tails." If you say "Heads," they must stop the ball and sit on it. If you say "Tails," they must stop the ball and then place their head on it. They must do this as quickly as possible. If you say "Change," the commands are switched so "heads" means they put their head on the ball and vice versa.

If players complete the command correctly they get a point, but if they do it incorrectly they lose a point. Give extra points to those who do it quickly and those who are dribbling quickly. If a girl's ball leaves adventure world or if it collides with another ball, the girl loses a point. The girl must spell her name with catch juggles before returning to the game.

The winner is the first girl to reach a set number of points.

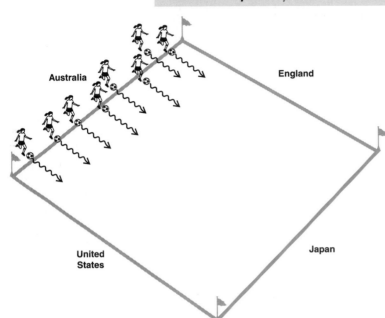
Around the World 3

Purpose: To improve dribbling skills and develop confidence while controlling a ball in a confined area
Number of Players: Any

Equipment: 1 ball per girl
Time: 5 to 10 minutes
Ages: 4 to 6

Australia

England

United States

Japan

Create an area 20 yards by 20 yards as your ocean. Each girl dribbles (sails) around the ocean with her soccer ball (boat). Each side of the area is named after a country: England, United States, Japan, and Australia. When a country name is called out, players must sail their soccer boats to that particular side as quickly as possible. When they arrive at each country, they must greet the people by performing an activity.

For example, when they reach England they must do five drag backs (see page 49) before setting sail again; when they reach the United States they must do five catch juggles (see page 59); when they reach Japan they must do five toe taps; and when they reach Australia they must flick the ball up off the ground and catch it in their hands.

Once again, be creative. You can have the girls shout out a phrase when they reach a particular country, such as saying "G'day, Mate" when they arrive at Australia. By adjusting the activities that need to be performed and by having the girls use both feet, the level of the game can be modified.

Kick Out 4

Purpose: To improve dribbling skills, develop an attacking mentality, and increase awareness of space in a confined area, with limited pressure

Number of Players: Any
Equipment: 1 ball per girl
Time: 5 to 10 minutes
Ages: 7 and up

Create an area 20 yards by 20 yards. Each girl dribbles around the area while keeping her ball under control and within the area. Select two girls to be the catchers based on who's working the hardest to perform a specific skill or move. The catchers have 1 minute to kick as many soccer balls out of the area as possible. If a girl's soccer ball is kicked out or leaves the area due to lack of control, she must perform a set number of juggles or a specific dribbling move five times before reentering the game. After 1 minute, count the number of girls outside the area. This is the kick-out score and the target to beat. Select several different girls to be the catchers and see which pair can reach the highest score.

Numbers Game 5

Purpose: To develop communication and organization skills and to encourage players to look up while dribbling	Number of Players: Any Equipment: 1 ball per girl Time: 3 to 5 minutes Ages: 7 and up

Create an area 20 yards by 20 yards. Each girl dribbles around the area while keeping her ball under control and in the area. While the girls are dribbling, the coach calls out a number, and the girls have to quickly get into groups of that number. The first group to form gets one point per player. Everybody dribbles again, and the coach calls out a different number. The girls once again have to quickly form groups of that number, with the first group getting one point each. Once the girls are comfortable communicating and getting themselves into groups, indicate the group size you want by holding up a specific number of fingers. Now the girls have to dribble around and keep control of the ball while keeping their head up.

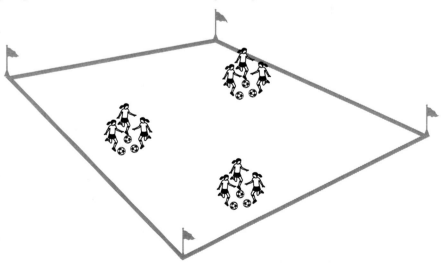

Shark Attack 6

Purpose: To improve the ability to change direction and beat a defender	**Equipment:** 1 ball per girl
	Time: 10 minutes
Number of Players: Any	**Ages:** 6 to 9

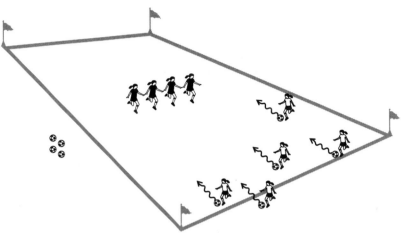

Create an area 30 yards long by 20 yards wide as the ocean. One side of the area is England and the other is the United States. On the command of "Shark attack," each girl attempts to dribble her ball (sail her boat) across the area (ocean) without getting caught by a shark. A player is caught if one of the sharks can place her foot on the ball. When players make it safely across the ocean, they must do five toe taps to secure their boat.

Initially the coach is the shark. Once a girl is caught, she places her soccer ball in a designated area away from the practice area and then becomes a shark.

The last girl to be caught is the winner and becomes the first shark for the next game.

Catch Me If You Can 7

Purpose: To improve dribbling, to practice changing direction, and to develop short passing techniques	**Equipment:** 1 ball per girl
	Time: 10 minutes
	Ages: 6 to 9
Number of Players: Any	

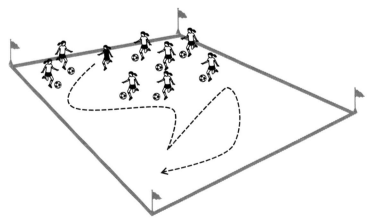

Create an area 20 yards by 20 yards as your adventure world. Each girl dribbles around and explores adventure world. On the command of "Catch me if you can," all the girls attempt to catch the coach. They chase you while dribbling, and when they're close enough they kick their soccer ball and try to hit you below the knees. Initially you can run very fast, but with each hit you lose energy and slow down. After the fifth hit you've lost all your energy.

You can no longer walk at all and fall to the ground. When this happens, the girls have defeated you and won the game.

Play the game a second time and select a girl to be on your team. Base this selection on who works hard for 30 seconds practicing a specific dribbling move. In this second game both the coach and the girl must be caught.

Great Bank Robbery 8

Purpose: To improve dribbling skills and to introduce moves to change direction and maintain possession **Number of Players:** 8 or more	**Equipment:** 8 or more soccer balls, 16 cones, and 4 flags for the bank **Time:** 10 minutes **Ages:** 6 to 9

Create an area 30 yards long by 20 yards wide as the city. Use the cones to mark out a small square in each corner to represent a hideout for each team. Divide the group into four teams. Give each team a name and send them to a hideout. In the middle of the area mark out another small square (the bank) and place all the soccer balls (the bags of money) inside. Each ball is valued at $100. On your command the teams run into the bank and, using their feet, attempt to take one ball back to their hide-

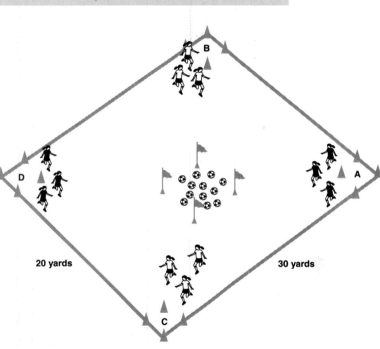

out. When all the balls have been removed from the bank, the girls are allowed to take balls from each other's hideouts. Each team can dribble only one ball at a time, and the girls are not allowed to guard their hideout. Balls can only be taken from the bank and the hideouts, not from other players. When the coach makes a siren-like noise, the alarm is raised, and all the players must return back to their hideouts within 5 seconds to avoid being caught by the police (the coach). If a player is caught, her team loses $200 from their hideout. Whichever team has the most money is the winner.

Progressions. The girls can only remove soccer balls by performing the drag-back move.

Introduce a distinctive colored ball that's worth $500.

Create one-on-one situations by allowing girls to take a ball from each other.

On Command 9

Purpose: To teach and develop dribbling skills used to change direction and beat defenders **Number of Players:** Any	**Equipment:** 1 ball per girl **Time:** 10 to 15 minutes **Ages:** 9 to 13

Create an area 20 yards by 20 yards. Each girl dribbles around the area, avoiding the other girls. Every three touches the girls change direction and change dribbling foot. On your command the girls must perform a specified move as fast as they can and accelerate into space. If you say "Step over," they must perform a step over. Call out as many different moves as the girls know. Introduce new moves if necessary. Continue the process but include "Left" or "Right" as part of the command. If you say "Left outside cut," the girls must perform an outside cut with the left foot.

Progressions. On your command the girls dribble and perform a specified move continuously for 30 seconds. They must have three touches between each move. Ask how many times they were able to perform the move and then challenge them to complete two more repetitions of the move in the same time period. On your command the players repeat the move for 30 seconds. Repeat the activity with different moves and then repeat it with the opposite foot.

The girls perform a specified move as in the first progression, but this time there's one girl without a ball. During the 30 seconds she must steal a ball from somebody else and perform the moves. If a player has her ball stolen, she then must steal a different soccer ball in order to continue.

Knock Out Five 10

Purpose: To improve dribbling skills in a restricted space against opponents
Number of Players: Any

Equipment: 1 ball per girl
Time: 10 to 15 minutes
Ages: 9 to 13

Create an area 20 yards by 20 yards. Each girl dribbles around the area, avoiding the other girls. On your command the girls attempt to knock each other's soccer ball out of the area. Once a girl's soccer ball has been knocked out, she must run after it as quickly as possible and collect it before it stops rolling. She must do 10 juggles and then quickly reenter the game. If the ball stops moving before the girl reaches it, she must perform 15 juggles before reentering. The first girl to knock out five soccer balls is the winner. Whenever a girl's ball is knocked out, her score goes back to zero.

Diagonal One-on-One 11

Purpose: To improve dribbling moves in a restricted space against a defender, with an emphasis on changing direction and speed
Number of Players: Any number in groups of 2

Equipment: 1 ball and 4 cones per group
Time: 3 minutes per game
Ages: 11 to 13

Use 4 cones to create a square 10 yards wide. One girl passes the ball diagonally across the square and becomes the defender as soon as her opponent takes her first touch. The receiving player becomes the attacker and must dribble and stop the ball at either of the cones at her side in order to score. As the defender moves to cover one side, the attacker must quickly perform a move to change direction and attack the space and the cone on the opposite side of the square. If the defender wins the ball, the roles are reversed.

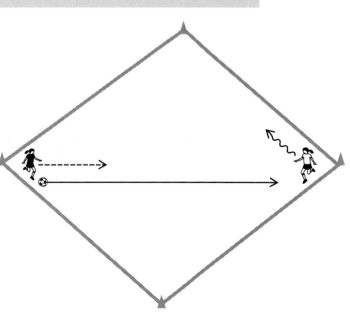

One-on-One to a Line 12

Purpose: To improve attacking dribbling moves in a restricted space in order to beat a defender **Number of Players:** Any number in groups of 2	**Equipment:** 1 ball and 4 cones per group **Time:** 3 minutes per game **Ages:** 11 to 13

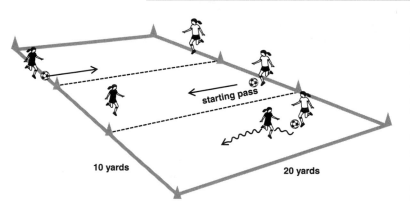

10 yards

20 yards

starting pass

Use the cones to create multiple one-on-one areas 10 yards wide by 20 yards long. One girl passes the ball to her opponent 20 yards away and becomes a defender. The receiving player becomes the attacker and must control the ball, dribble past the defender, and stop the ball on the defender's starting line. The defender attempts to steal the ball and stop it on the attacker's starting line. The first player to stop the ball on the opponent's starting line scores a point, and the roles are reversed. Place emphasis on performing an attacking dribbling move, changing direction, and changing speed to beat the defender.

Progression. Add bonus points if the attacker can score using specific dribbling moves.

Passing

Monsters, Inc. II 13

Purpose: To develop the technique of short passing with the inside of the foot **Number of Players:** Any number in groups of 2	**Equipment:** 1 ball per group **Time:** 10 minutes **Ages:** 4 to 6

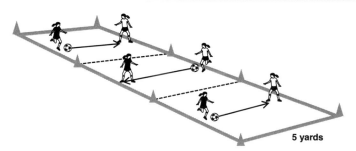

5 yards

This is a passing game based on the popular animated movie. Girls stand about 5–10 yards apart and try to pass the ball through their partners' legs using the inside of the foot. If they're successful, they get one scream point and must scream as loud as possible to collect it. They're attempting to collect as many screams as possible. They can collect scream points together or individually.

Progressions. Girls play the game using alternate feet.
Increase the distance between the two girls.

Stuck in the Mud 14

Purpose: To develop dribbling skills and short passing with the inside of the foot	**Equipment:** 1 ball per girl
	Time: 10 to 15 minutes
	Ages: 4 to 6
Number of Players: Any	

Create an area 20 yards by 20 yards as the swamp. The girls must dribble around and explore the swamp, keeping an eye open for the mud monster that resides in the area. If their soccer ball leaves the swamp, they must quickly spell their name with catch juggles (see page 59) to rejoin the game. The coach plays the role of the mud monster and attempts to stop each girl from playing soccer in the swamp. The mud monster tries to place a foot on the ball and push it 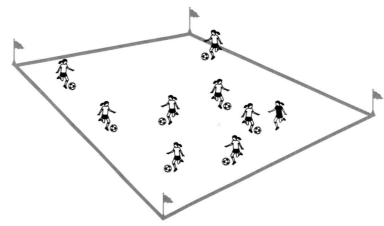 into the mud, so that the girl becomes stuck in the mud. Then she must hold the ball above her head with her legs apart and call to her teammates to save her. She can be saved only if a teammate passes a ball through her legs. Demonstrate the correct technique to pass the ball using the inside of the foot. The mud monster attempts to stop all the girls and win the game.

Play the game a second time, selecting two girls to be the mud monsters. All the girls will want to be the mud monster, so select two girls who've worked hard for 30 seconds practicing a specific dribbling move.

Progressions. Allow only the weak foot to be used to save those who are stuck in the mud.
Allow only a pass with the outside of the foot to be used to save those who are stuck in the mud.

Smelly Egg 15

Purpose: To develop and improve short passing with the inside of the foot	Equipment: 1 ball per girl and one different colored ball
	Time: 10 to 15 minutes
Number of Players: 8 or more	Ages: 4 to 6

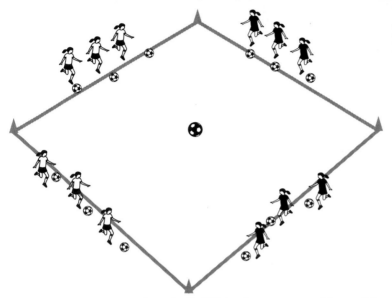

Create an area 15 yards by 15 yards as the egg farm. Divide the group into two teams and position each team around the outside of the area, so that each team covers two sides opposite the other team. Each girl has a ball. In the middle place a ball of a distinctive color, which is the smelly egg. Nobody wants the smelly egg on her side of the farm. Each girl attempts to pass her soccer ball so that it hits the egg and moves it in the direction of the opposite team. Once her ball has stopped moving she must run into the area, collect it, and dribble out, without being hit by a ball. If hit, she must quickly spell her name with catch juggles (see page 59) before continuing. The first team to send the smelly egg over the opposing team's line is the winner.

Progressions. Girls play the game passing the ball with alternate feet. Increase the size of the playing area.

Dog Pound 16

Purpose: To develop dribbling skills and short passing with the inside of the foot	Equipment: 6 soccer balls
	Time: 5 to 10 minutes
	Ages: 7 to 8
Number of Players: 8 or more	

Create an area 30 yards long by 20 yards wide as the dog pound. Split the group into two teams, the dogs and the dogcatchers. The dogs begin inside the area without a ball, and the dogcatchers begin outside the area with a ball. On your command the girls with the ball dribble into the dog pound and attempt to catch the dogs by passing the soccer ball and hitting them below the knee. When a girl has been caught, she must stand with her feet shoulder width apart and can be saved only if a teammate can crawl through her legs. To avoid anybody getting hit in the face with the ball, the dogcatchers can't catch dogs while the dogs are in the process of saving a teammate. The dogcatchers have 2 minutes to win the game by attempting to catch all the dogs. The roles are then reversed, with the dogcatchers becoming the dogs and vice versa. If neither team is able to catch all of the dogs in the set time, the team that catches the most dogs is the winner.

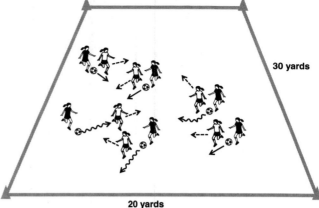

Progressions. Play the game using the weak foot to pass.

Play the game using the outside of the foot to pass.

Soccer Mall 17

Purpose: To develop and improve short passing with the inside of the foot while moving **Number of Players:** Any number in groups of 2	**Equipment:** 1 soccer ball per group and 12 to 16 cones **Time:** 10 to 15 minutes **Ages:** 7 to 8

Create an area 30 yards long by 20 yards wide as the shopping mall and randomly lay out a series of small gates that act as the shops. The gates are 3 yards wide. Working in groups of two players, the girls pass and move around the mall and attempt to be the first pair to buy something at every shop (players can move randomly around the shops and don't have to visit them in a set order). When they arrive at a shop they must make five consecutive passes

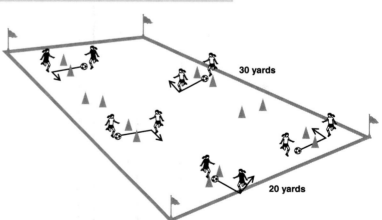

to buy an item. After the first round it's fun for the girls to tell you some of the items they bought from each shop. Repeat in the opposite direction, with the girls playing passes with the opposite foot.

Progressions. In the second round the girls only have to play two passes through each gate in order to buy something, but they can have just four touches of the ball between each shop. Repeat using passes with alternate feet. Teach the girls to control the ball in the direction they want to go and to pass the ball in front of their partner.

Progress the game relative to ability, so that the players make one pass at each gate and are allowed just two touches of the ball between gates. Repeat the game with girls playing passes with the opposite foot.

Tunnel Run 18

Purpose: To improve the accuracy and timing of short passing with the inside of the foot **Number of Players:** 8 or more	**Equipment:** 1 ball per girl **Time:** 10 to 15 minutes **Ages:** 7 to 8

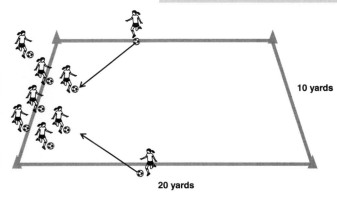

10 yards

20 yards

Create an area 20 yards long by 10 yards wide as the tunnel. The width of the area can be adjusted to make the game easier or harder. On your command of "Tunnel Run," all the girls at once attempt to dribble through the tunnel from one end to the other, without their ball getting hit. To prevent the girls from just kicking and running after the ball, explain that they're to have at least eight touches of the ball when running through the tunnel. Select two girls who are the tunnel police. They stand outside the area and pass their soccer ball to hit those dribbling through. When a girl's ball is hit, she collects it quickly and joins the tunnel police on either side of the area. The last person to get hit wins the tunnel run and becomes the first policewoman for the next game.

Progressions. Play the game again but with the tunnel police using alternate feet to pass the ball. Increase the difficulty by making the tunnel wider.

Soccer Tennis 19

Purpose: To improve short passing and develop good first touch **Number of Players:** Any number in groups of 2	**Equipment:** 1 ball and 2 cones per group **Time:** 3 to 5 minutes per game **Ages:** 9 to 12

Create an area 10 yards by 10 yards as a tennis court, and in the middle use the cones to create a small gate 3 yards wide. One girl begins by passing the ball on the ground through the gate to her opponent on the other side. Using two touches, the receiving girl must control the ball and pass it back through. The rules are simple: the ball must stay inside the court, must re-

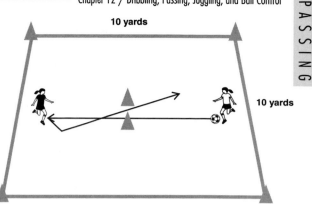

main on the ground, and must be moving at all times. If one girl is unable to pass through the gate or breaks a rule, then the other girl is awarded one point. After 5 minutes of play, whoever has the most points wins the game.

Progression. Increasing the length of the court or decreasing the width of the gate will increase the difficulty of the game and further improve the accuracy and distance of the passing.

Numbered Passing 20

Purpose: To improve passing over short and medium distances using different surfaces of the feet, while also developing first touch and communication	**Number of Players:** 12 **Equipment:** 4 balls **Time:** 10 to 15 minutes **Ages:** 9 to 12

Divide the team into two groups, and give each girl a number from 1 to 6. Each group has one ball and must pass in numbered order: player 1 passes to 2, 2 passes to 3, 3 passes to 4, 4 passes to 5, 5 passes to 6, and then 6 passes to 1. That is one round of passes. The competition is a race to be the first group to complete 10 rounds.

If the group doesn't pass in order, if the ball stops moving, or if anybody is stationary, then the group must start over. Communication is essential to succeed, so encourage the girls to call for the ball when it is their turn to receive the pass.

Progressions. Create an area 20 yards by 20 yards that each group must stay in. Also reduce the number of touches each girl is allowed. If the ball leaves the area or if a girl has too many touches, the group must start over. Build up to playing with no more than two touches. Emphasize the importance of accuracy of the passes and also the timing and weight of each pass.

Once the group is able to complete 10 rounds using just two touches, add a second ball. At the start, player 1 and player 3 each have a ball. Now timing, movement off the ball, communication, accuracy, and first touch become vital.

Keep-Away 21

Purpose: To develop ball control and passing over short distances using different surfaces of the feet while under pressure from a defender	**Number of Players:** 5 **Equipment:** 1 ball **Time:** 10 minutes **Ages:** 9 to 12

Create a square 12 yards by 12 yards. Four girls have to keep the ball away from one defender for as long as possible. Every time the ball leaves the area due to a poor pass or poor control, the defender gets one point. She also gets a point every time she gains possession of the ball. When the defender reaches five points her time is up, and she switches with another player. Placing emphasis on the defender to work hard and win the ball back quickly creates a situation where the girls are forced to practice at their technical edge. This learning environment of being pressured into making mistakes leads to a faster rate of development.

Progressions. With weaker groups of players, increase the size of the area and restrict the defender to walking.

With stronger groups of players, reduce the size of the area and the number of touches each girl is allowed on the ball.

Long Passing Gates 22

Purpose: To develop longer-range passing **Number of Players:** Any number in groups of 2	**Equipment:** 1 ball and 4 cones per group **Time:** 3 to 5 minutes per game **Ages:** 11 and up

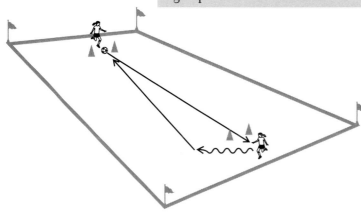

Use the cones to create two gates 25 yards apart, with each gate 5 yards wide. The girls compete in pairs against each other for 5 minutes. The girl starting the game passes the ball through her opponent's gate. The second girl must control the ball, move it out to the side of her gate, and pass the ball back through her opponent's gate. If either girl misses the gate or has more than two touches, or if the ball stops moving, her opponent gets one point. The girl with the most points after 5 minutes is the winner. Everybody plays three games against different opponents.

Progressions. Increase the distance between the gates and decrease the width of each gate to further challenge the length and accuracy of the long-range pass.

Encourage the girls to develop a more advanced lofted pass by stating that the ball must pass through the gates in the air.

Four-on-Two Competition 23

Purpose: To improve passing accuracy, weight, and timing while maintaining possession of the ball **Number of Players:** 12	**Equipment:** 2 balls and 6 cones **Time:** 10 to 15 minutes **Ages:** 12 and up

Use the cones to create two squares, each 20 yards by 20 yards. Divide the group into teams of six players, with a team in each square. Two girls from each team put on bibs and go into the other area to defend for 4 minutes. Every time the ball leaves the area due to a poor pass or loss of control, the defenders get a point for their team. They also get a point every time they gain possession of the ball and make two passes.

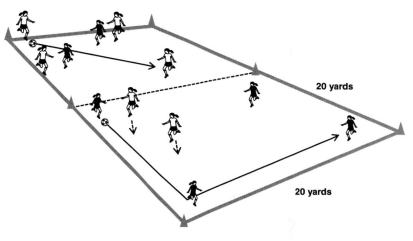

20 yards

20 yards

After 4 minutes the defenders return to their original group and switch with two other girls. When everybody has spent 4 minutes defending, the team with the most points is the winner. Placing emphasis on the defenders to gain points creates a realistic situation where the girls are forced to practice at their technical edge.

In this four-on-two situation girls are able to practice the technique of playing short and longer passes with accuracy, speed, and disguise. In addition, ball control, first touch, and decision making are also developed.

Progression. With stronger groups reduce the size of the playing area and the number of touches each girl is allowed on the ball.

Juggling

Catch Juggles 24

Purpose: To develop basic foot and hand coordination with a ball	**Equipment:** 1 ball per girl
	Time: 3 to 5 minutes
Number of Players: Any	**Ages:** 4 to 6

A girl starts with the ball in her hands at waist height. She drops the ball, and before it hits the ground she must kick it back up into the air using the instep of the foot and catch it in her hands. That is a catch juggle. Girls attempt to see how many catch juggles they can do without the ball hitting the ground.

Name Juggling 25

Purpose: To develop basic foot and hand coordination with a ball	**Equipment:** 1 ball per girl
	Time: 3 to 5 minutes
Number of Players: Any	**Ages:** 4 to 6

Girls attempt to spell their name with catch juggles. Each girl does a catch juggle by dropping her ball and kicking it into the air before it hits the ground. Then the girl says the first letter of her name. She does a second catch juggle and then says the second letter of her name. She continues until she has spelled her name, but if the ball hits the ground she must start again.

Bounce Juggling 26

Purpose: To develop basic foot coordination with the ball and basic ball control in the air	**Equipment:** 1 ball per girl
	Time: 3 to 5 minutes
	Ages: 7 to 8
Number of Players: Any	

A girl starts with the ball in her hands at waist height. She drops the ball and allows it to bounce on the ground. Before the ball hits the ground a second time, she must kick it back up into the air using the instep of the foot. That is one bounce juggle. The ball is allowed to bounce again before every juggle. Girls attempt to see how many bounce juggles they can do before the ball hits the ground twice in a row.

Catch Juggling II 27

Purpose: To improve basic foot coordination with the ball and develop juggling and ball control in the air	**Number of Players:** Any **Equipment:** 1 ball per girl **Time:** 3 to 5 minutes **Ages:** 7 to 8

A girl starts with the ball in her hands at waist height. She must do one juggle with any part of her body and catch the ball. That's catch one juggle. She must then do two consecutive juggles before catching it. That's catch two juggles. She must then do three consecutive juggles before catching it. That's catch three juggles. Girls attempt to see how high they can go. As soon as the ball hits the ground they must start again with one juggle.

Total Body Juggling 28

Purpose: To develop overall ball control in the air using the entire body **Number of Players:** Any	**Equipment:** 1 ball per girl **Time:** 3 to 5 minutes **Ages:** 7 to 8

Starting with the ball on the ground, girls attempt to juggle the ball for as long as possible using only the feet, thighs, and head. Once a girl completes eight touches of the ball before it hits the ground, she's completed eight juggles.

Feet-Only Juggling 29

Purpose: To improve ball control in the air using just the feet **Number of Players:** Any	**Equipment:** 1 ball per girl **Time:** 3 to 5 minutes **Ages:** 9 to 10

Starting with the ball on the ground, girls see how many juggles they can complete using only their feet.

Thigh-Only Juggling 30

Purpose: To improve ball control in the air using just the thighs **Number of Players:** Any	**Equipment:** 1 ball per girl **Time:** 3 to 5 minutes **Ages:** 9 to 10

Starting with the ball in the hands, girls see how many juggles they can complete using only their thighs.

Juggling to the Goal 31

Purpose: To improve control of the ball so that a player can move around while controlling the ball in the air **Number of Players:** Any	**Equipment:** 1 ball per girl **Time:** 3 to 5 minutes **Ages:** 9 to 10

Starting on the edge of the penalty area, girls attempt to juggle the ball to the 6-yard area and then score with a volley on the goal.

Partner Juggling 32

Purpose: To improve the control of a ball arriving in the air at different heights using any part of the body **Number of Players:** Any in groups of 2	**Equipment:** 1 ball per group **Time:** 5 minutes **Ages:** 11 to 12

Working in pairs, girls see how many juggles they can complete together without the ball hitting the ground. The maximum number of juggles in a row that each girl can complete before passing the ball to her partner is 10.

Sequential Feet Juggling 33

Purpose: To improve controlling the ball with a specific purpose using just the feet **Number of Players:** Any	**Equipment:** 1 ball per girl **Time:** 5 minutes **Ages:** 11 to 12

Starting with the ball on the ground, girls attempt to complete a sequence of juggles using only their feet. The sequence goes as follows: do one juggle with the right foot and one with the left foot, then two juggles with the right and two with the left, three with the right and three with the left, four with the right and four with the left. Players continue on as high as they can go. When the ball hits the ground, they must start over.

Ball Control

Pumpkin Picking 34

Purpose: To improve ball control in the air and on the ground **Number of Players:** Any	**Equipment:** 1 ball per girl **Time:** 10 to 15 minutes **Ages:** 7 to 8

Create an area 20 yards by 20 yards as your pumpkin patch. Each girl dribbles her ball around the patch and, on your command, must stop and pick pumpkins. To pick a mini-pumpkin, a girl holds the ball in her hands and drops it to the ground from knee height. As the ball hits the ground the girl must redirect it to the side without bouncing it, using the inside or outside of the foot. She then dribbles away and has five touches before picking another mini-pumpkin. If the ball bounces or stops under her feet when controlling it, that pumpkin is crushed and can't be counted. After 60 seconds the girl who has picked the most mini-pumpkins is the winner. Play several times, changing which foot and what part of the foot the girls must use to control the ball as it hits the ground.

Progressions. Once the girls can control a ball dropped from knee height without it bouncing, they progress to controlling a ball dropped from waist height. They're now picking large pumpkins. Once again, see how many pumpkins they can pick in 60 seconds.

Finally, the girls can try to pick giant pumpkins. The ball must be thrown into the air above head height before being redirected to the side without bouncing as it hits the ground.

First-Touch Races 35

Purpose: To improve first touch and ball control on the ground	Equipment: 2 balls per group
Number of Players: Any in groups of 2	**Time:** 5 to 10 minutes **Ages:** 7 to 9

Working in groups of two players, the girls stand 15 yards apart. One girl is the server and the other the receiver. It's a race to be the first pair to get 10 points. The server starts with both soccer balls and passes the first to her partner. With her first touch, the receiver must control the ball to the side at a distance of no more than 2 yards. The server then passes the second ball to her partner. In order to score a point, the receiver must redirect the second ball with her first touch to hit the first ball. Roles are then reversed; the receiver becomes the server and vice versa.

Progression. Change the foot that's used to take the first touch and then repeat the activity using the outside of the foot.

Control Gates 36

Purpose: To improve first touch and ball control on the ground using different surfaces of the feet **Number of Players:** Any in groups of 2	**Equipment:** 1 ball and 4 cones per group **Time:** 10 to 15 minutes **Ages:** 7 to 10

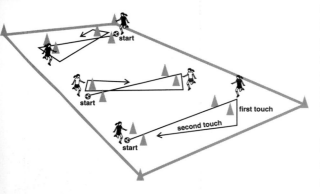

Use the cones to create two small gates 10 yards apart. The gates should be about 2 yards wide. Girls are placed in groups of two players and play opposite each other. The server passes the ball on the ground through both gates to start the game. The receiver must control the ball to the side of her gate (not through it) with her first touch, and then she passes the ball back through her opponent's gate with her second touch.

Each girl must control the ball to the side of her gate (not through it) and then pass the ball back on the ground through her opponent's gate using only two touches and without the ball stopping. If she misses the gate, has more than two touches, passes the ball in the air, or allows the ball to stop moving, then her opponent gets one point. The girls play for 4 minutes and then switch partners. If playing the game with two touches is too difficult for your team, allow three touches.

Progressions. Once your players have the concept of how and where to control the ball and can play the game with two touches, focus on the different kinds of first touch. First they must use the right foot to control to the right side of the gate and use the left foot to control to the left side of the gate. Next they use the left foot to control to the right side and the right foot to control to the left side.

To improve the girls' control with the outside of the foot, play the game with the restriction that they must take their first touch with the outside of the foot.

Stop and Go 37

Purpose: To improve controlling the ball out of the air and onto the ground quickly and efficiently in a competitive environment	**Number of Players:** Any **Equipment:** 1 ball per girl **Time:** 10 to 15 minutes **Ages:** 9 to 12

Create an area 20 yards by 20 yards. Divide the girls into groups of two players and have them number themselves 1 or 2. Player 1 in each group has 60 seconds to tag her partner on the shoulder (with her hand) as many times as possible. Both girls must dribble around the area with the ball at their feet at all times. If the girl being chased leaves the area, her partner automatically gets three tags. If the girl doing the tagging leaves the area, she automatically loses three tags.

On your command "Stop," both girls must stop exactly where they are and flick the ball up into their hands. On the command "Go," both girls must throw the ball above their head and control the ball without it bouncing. Player 1 must control the ball toward her partner in order to catch and tag her, while player 2 must control the ball into space away from her partner to avoid being tagged. Shout "Stop" or "Go" about five times during the 60 seconds.

Roles are then reversed, and play resumes. The girl with the most tags is the winner.

Three-on-One World Cup 38

Purpose: To develop good ball control and first touch in a restricted area while being pressured by a defender **Number of Players:** 12	**Equipment:** 1 ball and 4 cones per group **Time:** 15 to 20 minutes **Ages:** 9 to 12

Use the cones to create three squares 12 yards by 12 yards in size. Split the group into three teams of four girls and place each team in a square. Each team represents a Women's World Cup soccer team, USA, Brazil, and China. China sends a player to defend against USA, USA sends a player to defend against Brazil, and Brazil sends a player to defend against China. Each team has to keep the ball away from the defender for 3 minutes.

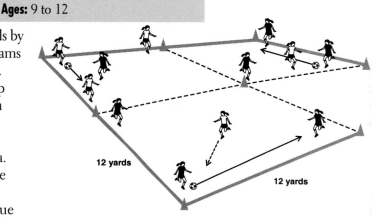

12 yards

12 yards

Every time the ball leaves the area due to a poor pass or loss of control, the defender gets one goal for her country. The defender also scores one goal every time she gets possession of the ball. After 3 minutes each defender returns to her home country, and another girl becomes the defender. Each girl defends for 3 minutes. When all four players have defended, the team with the most goals is the World Cup winner.

Air Control 39

Purpose: To improve first touch and ball control out of the air using the foot, thigh, chest, and head **Number of Players:** 8 or more	**Equipment:** 1 ball for every 2 girls **Time:** 15 to 20 minutes **Ages:** 11 and above

Create an area 20 yards by 20 yards. Position half the team with soccer balls around the outside of the area as the feeders. The other girls are inside the area and have 60 seconds to control as many balls in the air as possible. If a ball hits the ground or doesn't go back to the feeders' hands, it doesn't count

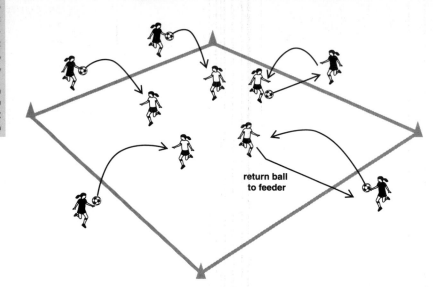

return ball
to feeder

as being controlled. The girls switch positions after 60 seconds and play the game again.

Progressions. Air Control 1: Control the ball with the thigh and pass it back with the foot. Air Control 2: Control the ball with the foot and pass it back with the foot. Air Control 3: Control the ball with the chest and pass it back with the foot. Air Control 4: Control the ball with the right thigh and pass it back with the left foot. Air Control 5: Control the ball with the right foot and pass it back with the left foot.

Control Squares 40

Purpose: To improve first touch and ball control on the ground using different surfaces of the feet in a restricted area **Number of Players:** Any in groups of 2	**Equipment:** 1 ball and 8 cones per group **Time:** 10 to 15 minutes **Ages:** 11 and above

Use the cones to create two small squares 15 yards apart. The squares should be about 3 yards by 3 yards in size. Girls play opposite each other and must take their first touch inside the square. One girl in each group is the server and passes the ball on the ground through the front of the square to start the game. The receiver controls the ball out the side of the square and then passes the ball back into her opponent's square through the front. The pass doesn't need to be on the ground, but it must be below head height. If the pass isn't on target, if a girl has more than two touches, or if the ball stops moving, then the receiver gets one point. Play for 4 minutes and then switch partners. (See Control Gates, page 152, which has the same setup except two additional cones are added to turn each gate into a square.)

Progression. Change the size of the squares and the distance between them to increase the level of difficulty.

Shooting and Finishing, and Heading

Shooting and Finishing

Monster Strike 41

Purpose: To teach and develop striking the ball using the instep	**Equipment:** 1 ball per group
	Time: 10 minutes
Number of Players: Any number in groups of 2	**Ages:** 4 to 6

This is a shooting game based on the theme of the popular animated movie. Each girl is trying to collect as many screams as possible by striking the ball through her partner's legs.

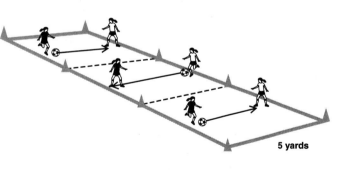

5 yards

The girls stand about 5–10 yards apart and take turns trying to strike the ball through their partner's legs using the instep of the foot. If a girl is successful she gets one scream point and must scream as loud as possible to collect it. Girls can collect scream points together or individually.

Progressions. Girls play the game using alternate feet.
   Increase the distance between the two girls.

Mickey and Minnie 42

Purpose: To develop the technique of striking the ball using the instep while stationary Number of Players: 8 or more	Equipment: 1 ball per girl and 12–14 cones Time: 10 to 15 minutes Ages: 4 to 6

Create two lines of cones 10 yards apart. Use the Numbers Game (see Game 5 on page 135) to split the group into two teams. One team is called Mickey Mouse and stands behind one line of cones; the other team is called Minnie Mouse and stands behind the other line of cones. The line of cones represents the bricks of a house. Once either Mickey or Minnie loses all the bricks in his or her house, the game is over.

Each girl stands behind the line of cones, shoots her soccer ball using her laces, and attempts to knock down one of the cones of the other team. Girls aren't allowed to stand in front of their cones in order to protect them and block shots. Once they've taken a shot, the girls don't run after their own ball but instead collect a ball that's been shot at their cones by the other team. The first team to knock over all the cones of the other team is the winner.

Progressions. Girls play the game alternating kicking with the right foot and the left foot.

Increase the distance between the two lines of cones.

Emergency 43

Purpose: To develop the technique of striking the ball using the instep while dribbling Number of Players: 8 or more	Equipment: 1 ball per girl, 8 cones, and 4 flags (cones can be used in place of flags) Time: 10 to 15 minutes Ages: 4 to 6

Use the flags to create an area 30 yards long by 20 yards wide as the hospital. With the cones, set up a small square at each end as the emergency room. Divide the group into two teams and have one team wear bibs. Everybody dribbles around the hospital with a soccer ball, avoiding players from the other team. Select the girl who's working the hardest from each team to be a doctor. Each doctor begins without a ball inside the small square (the emergency room). On your command girls from both teams attempt to shoot the balls and hit the legs of anyone from the other team. Once a girl has been struck, she must quickly collect her ball and kneel down holding the ball above her head, shouting "Emergency, emergency." As soon as the doctor sees that one of her teammates has been struck, she runs out of the small square and saves the girl by tapping the top of her soccer ball. Once saved, the girl can get up and continue to dribble around and try to hit the other team. The doctor must run back to the ER without getting hit. The first team to strike the opposing doctor in the legs with the ball when she is out of the ER is the winner.

30 yards

20 yards

Rapid Fire 44

Purpose: To improve shooting and the technique of striking the ball while attempting to score on goal **Number of Players:** 12	**Equipment:** 4 balls, 4 cones, and 5 flags (cones can be used in place of flags) **Time:** 15 to 20 minutes **Ages:** 7 to 10

Use the flags to set up four goals alongside each other. Divide the girls into groups of three, with each girl numbering herself 1, 2, or 3. Player 1 goes into the goal as the goalkeeper, while players 2 and 3 stand as strikers on either side of the goal 15 yards away. The two strikers have a 5-minute rapid-fire round to see how many goals they can score. Begin by having the girls strike a stationary ball. If the goalkeeper saves a shot, she turns and rolls the ball in the opposite direction to the other striker. After a girl scores or misses, her partner must first retrieve the ball before taking a shot. Rotate the goalkeeper after 5 minutes. Once every player has had a turn in the goal, the girl with the most goals is the winner.

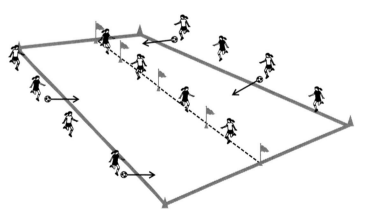

Progressions. Girls pass the ball out ahead of their body and strike it while it is moving away from them.

Using the hands, girls throw the ball out in front of their body and strike it after the first bounce.

The keeper passes the ball to the attacker who strikes it with one touch.

Street Soccer 45

Purpose: To develop an attacking mentality, create goal-scoring opportunities, and improve shooting and finishing in a competitive environment	**Number of Players:** Any number in groups of 3 **Equipment:** 1 ball per group **Time:** 10 to 15 minutes **Ages:** 8 to 12

In every country around the world, kids learn to play soccer without the direction of adults. A game of street soccer replicates these conditions and develops shooting and finishing within a fun competitive environment.

Split the team into groups of three. It's a race to see which group is the first to be playing street soccer. Direct each group to number themselves 1, 2, and 3 as quickly as possible. Players 1 and 2 get a bag or jacket each and make a goal, while player 3 gets a ball and becomes the goalkeeper. Players 1 and 2 compete against each other to score. The first girl to score two goals is the winner and becomes the new goalkeeper. A new game begins, and the action is continuous, with each girl trying to win the most games.

Progressions. Introduce a shooting line 10 yards from the goal. For a goal to count, the ball must be shot from behind this line.

Play the game in groups of four, so that the girl with the ball has to beat two defenders before shooting and scoring.

Four-Goal World Cup 46

Purpose: To develop an attacking mentality, create goal-scoring opportunities, and improve shooting and finishing in a competitive team environment	**Number of Players:** 12 **Equipment:** 4 balls and 8 flags (cones can be used in place of flags) **Time:** 10 to 15 minutes **Ages:** 9 and older

Use the flags to create an area 40 yards by 40 yards, and set up a goal on each of the four sides. Divide the group into teams of three players. Each team selects a country to represent and defends one goal. Using two or three balls in play at once, each team attempts to score on any of the other teams. Each team begins with five points, but every time a goal is conceded they lose a point. Once a team has lost all its points, the game is over. The team that has the most points at the end is the Women's World Cup winner.

Two-on-One to the Goal 47

Purpose: To develop goal-scoring opportunities through combination play and individual attacking skills, and to improve shooting and finishing when under pressure	**Number of Players:** 10 **Equipment:** 6 balls, 6 cones, and 4 flags (cones can be used in place of flags) **Time:** 10 to 15 minutes **Ages:** 9 to 11

Use the flags to create three large gates, each 12 yards wide, in an arc on the edge of the penalty area. Use the cones to set up three small (3 feet wide) target goals 20 yards from each gate. Divide the girls into groups of three players, with all groups playing at once toward the single main goal. Select one girl to be the goalkeeper. In each group, a defender starts at the gate, and two attackers start at the small target goal. The game begins with the defender passing to either of the two attackers (1). The two attackers try to beat the defender through the large gate and to score on the main goal (2). Emphasis should be placed on

using both combination play and individual dribbling to beat the defender. Encourage each second attacker to make runs on goal and both attackers to attempt a variety of finishes when in front of the goal. The defender tries to stop the attackers from scoring, win back possession of the ball, and score on the small target goal (3). Rotate the defender every 3 minutes.

Shooting Squares 48

Purpose: To improve various shooting and finishing techniques from the edge of the penalty area **Number of Players:** 8 or more **Equipment:** 1 ball per girl, 2 cones, and	8 flags (cones can be used in place of flags) **Time:** 10 to 15 minutes **Ages:** 10 to 12

Use the flags to set up two small squares on the top of the penalty area and place a starting cone 5 yards away. Select one girl to be the goalkeeper and divide the rest of the group into two teams that will compete against each other to see who can score the most goals. One girl must keep count of her team's goals. Each team begins behind the starting cone. The first girl jogs into the square and turns her body sideways to receive a short pass from the second girl. She must control the ball, take her first touch out the side of the square, and then shoot on her second touch. After her shot this girl quickly collects the ball and returns to the starting cone to play a pass to a teammate.

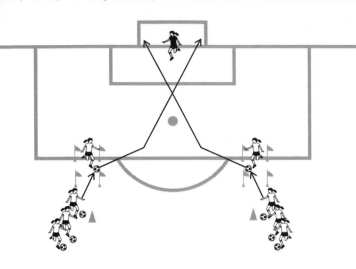

Play continues, with the girls taking turns at shooting on goal. In the first round the girls control the ball near the middle of the field as they move toward the goal. After 3 minutes both teams quickly switch shooting squares so that they're using the opposite foot. Award a bonus goal to the first team ready each time they switch sides. If you have more than eight girls at practice, increase the number of shooting opportunities by setting up three shooting squares and using three teams.

Progressions. The girls control the ball inside.
The girls control the ball outside.
Award double points for goals scored in the far corner.
The girls feed the pass in the air and finish with a volley or scissors kick.

One-on-One to the Goal 49

Purpose: To improve the attacking skills used to beat defenders, create goal-scoring opportunities, and improve shooting technique under pressure	Number of Players: Any number in groups of 2 Equipment: 1 ball per group and 12 cones Time: 10 to15 minutes Ages: 11 and above

The attacker must first beat the defender and then attempt to score on the goal.

The setup is similar to that used in Two-on-One to the Goal (see Game 47 on page 159). Create a series of large gates, 12 yards wide, in an arc on the edge of the penalty area. Set up a series of small target goals 20 yards from each gate. Girls work in groups of two players, with everybody playing at once toward the single main goal. Select one girl to be the goalkeeper. The game begins with the defender in each group passing to the attacker. The attacker tries to dribble past the defender through the gate and to score on the main goal. The defender tries to steal the ball and to score on the small target goal. The girls switch roles every time a goal is scored. After 3 minutes, the girl who has scored the most goals is the winner.

Close-Range Finishing 50

Purpose: To improve close-range finishing and develop a goal-scoring mentality inside the penalty area	**Equipment:** 12 balls
	Time: 15 to 20 minutes
	Ages: 11 and above
Number of Players: 12	

Position four girls around the outside of the penalty area as the feeders. Give each feeder a number—1, 2, 3, or 4—and three soccer balls each. Select one girl to be the goalkeeper in the goal and one to be the ball collector behind the goal. (The ball collector passes the balls back to the feeders to make sure they always have a supply of soccer balls.) The remaining players pair up to create three teams of strikers. The strikers aren't allowed outside the penalty area. When you call out a number, the feeder with that number must pass a ball to an open player or cross into the 6-yard area. The three teams compete against each other to finish every ball and score. The team that scores the most goals is the winner. Rotate the girls every 5 minutes. Encourage the girls to use a variety of surfaces and techniques for their shots and to develop a scorer's mentality in front of the goal.

Heading

Zoo Time 51

Purpose: To develop dribbling skills and introduce confidence using the head	**Equipment:** 1 ball per girl
	Time: 3 to 5 minutes
	Ages: 4 to 6
Number of Players: Any	

This is a fun adventure game to introduce heading to beginners. Create an area 20 yards by 20 yards as the zoo. The girls must dribble around and explore the zoo with the soccer ball. Each side of the area is the home of a different animal: monkeys, seals, giraffes, and elephants. When an animal name is called out, the girls must dribble to that particular side of the zoo as quickly as possible and demonstrate that animal's trick.

The seals like to balance the ball on their head; the giraffes like to balance the ball on the back of their neck; the elephants like to use their trunks (head) to dribble around; and the monkeys like to juggle the ball using their head. While the girls are performing each animal's trick, they can also mimic the sounds the animals make.

Finally, if you call out "Ostriches," the players have to pretend to bury their heads in the sand by placing their head on the soccer ball.

Crossing the River 52

Purpose: To develop basic heading technique and build confidence when heading the ball	**Equipment:** 1 ball per group and 12 cones
	Time: 3 to 5 minutes
Number of Players: Any number in groups of 2	**Ages:** 4 to 6

Create two lines of cones just 2 yards apart to serve as the river. The girls work in groups of two players and see how many times they can get the ball back and forth across the river using just their heads. One girl begins by holding the ball in her hands at eye level. Keeping her eyes open she heads the ball out of her hands and across the river to her partner. Her teammate must catch the ball without it hitting the ground and then attempt to head it back over. Players have 3 minutes to see how many consecutive times they can get the ball across the river.

Progression. Once the girls are comfortable heading the ball out of their own hands, progress to their throwing the ball up in the air and then heading it over the river.

Head Catch Juggling 53

Purpose: To develop ball control using the head and build confidence when heading the ball	**Equipment:** 1 ball per girl
	Time: 3 to 5 minutes
	Ages: 7 to 8
Number of Players: Any	

Each girl starts with the ball in her hands and throws it above her head. Using her forehead, she heads the ball back into the air before catching it with her hands. That is one head catch juggle. She must then do two consecutive headers before catching the ball; then she does three headers, and so on. The girls see how high they can go. As soon as the ball hits the ground, they must start again with one head catch juggle.

Heading Races 54

Purpose: To head the ball with greater accuracy and increased power	**Equipment:** 1 ball per group and 12 cones
Number of Players: Any number in groups of 2	**Time:** 3 to 5 minutes
	Ages: 7 to 8

Create two lines of cones 5 yards apart. The girls, working in groups of two, stand opposite each other, behind the lines of cones and race to be the first pair to complete 10 headers each. The first girl feeds the ball underarm to her partner, who is 5 yards away and who heads it straight back. The feeder must catch the ball without it hitting the ground. If the ball hits the ground, that header doesn't count. After five feeds, they switch roles. The girls continue to switch every 5 headers. The first pair to successfully complete 10 headers each is the winner.

Progression. Increase the distance between the two girls and play again.

Heads Up 55

Purpose: To head the ball over greater distances with greater power	**Equipment:** 1 ball per group and 12 cones
Number of Players: Any number in groups of 2	**Time:** 3 to 5 minutes
	Ages: 8 to 10

This is a great game for developing more powerful headers and for getting the girls to use their entire body when heading the ball. Create two end lines 40 yards apart. The length of the end lines is determined by the number of players. Divide the group into pairs and position them facing one another halfway between the end lines. The girls initially stand 5 yards apart. The game begins with the first girl throwing the ball to herself and heading it as far forward as possible. The receiving player lets the ball bounce, catches it, and then heads it back as far as possible in the opposite direction. Each girl attempts to drive her partner backward until she steps over the end line.

Partner Head Catch 56

Purpose: To improve heading accuracy and learn to pass the ball using the head	**Equipment:** 1 ball per group
	Time: 3 to 5 minutes
	Ages: 9 and older
Number of Players: Any number in groups of 2	

The girls work in groups of two players. One girl feeds the ball underarm to her partner, who is 5 yards away and who heads it straight back for the first girl to catch. The second time the first girl feeds the ball, her partner heads it back, and then the first girl heads it back for her partner to catch. They then try to do three headers back and forth before catching the ball, followed by four headers and so on. If the ball hits the ground, the pair starts again from the beginning.

Progression. Once the girls get to 10 head catches, they see how many times they can head the ball back and forth in the air without it hitting the ground.

Heading Wars 57

Purpose: To introduce and develop diving headers	Equipment: 1 ball and 4 cones per group
Number of Players: Any number in groups of 2	**Time:** 5 to 10 minutes
	Ages: 9 to 10

This is a great way to introduce girls to diving headers. Use the cones to create two small goals 8 yards apart. Each goal should be 4 yards wide. The girls are opposite each other in front of the goals. Each girl begins on her knees and feeds the ball to her partner. The receiving player attempts to head the ball past her partner into the goal. The feed must be in front of the girl so that she has to fall forward onto her hands in order to head the ball.

Progressions. If the girl who feeds the ball can head back her partner's header and score, the goal is worth double.

Move the girls from a kneeling position to a crouching position and then to a standing position as their confidence builds. Increase the distance between the two goals.

Two-on-Two Heading 58

Purpose: To encourage girls to attack through the ball when heading and to improve both offensive and defensive headers	Equipment: 1 ball and 4 flags (cones can be used in place of flags)
	Time: 10 to 15 minutes
	Ages: 9 to 12
Number of Players: 4	

Use the flags to create two goals 15 yards apart. The goals should be 8 yards wide. Divide the group into teams of two players. One girl from team A moves to the side of the area and feeds the ball in the air for her partner to try and head past team B. A girl from team B then collects the ball, moves to the side, and sets up her partner for a header. The team defending can either catch or head the ball. If the ball is caught, the game continues with a quick feed from the side. If the defending team heads the ball straight back and scores, the goal is worth double. To practice attacking headers, only allow goals to be scored below head height; to practice defensive headers, only allow goals to be scored above head height. Goals can only be scored from headers.

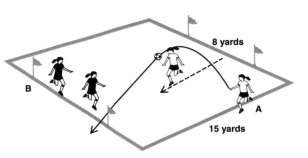

Progression. As the girls gain more confidence and improve their technique, further increase the distance between the two goals.

Attacking Headers 59

Purpose: To improve attacking headers and goal scoring using the head	**Equipment:** 1 ball per group and 4 flags (cones can be used in place of flags)
Number of Players: Any number in groups of 3	**Time:** 10 to 15 minutes
	Ages: 11 and above

Use the flags to set up goals alongside each other. Use the Numbers Game (see Game 5 on page 135) to get the girls into groups of three players, with each girl numbering herself 1, 2, or 3. Player 1 goes into the goal as the goalkeeper while players 2 and 3 stand on either side of the goal 10 yards away as the attackers. The two attackers have 5 minutes to see how many headers they can score. The goalkeeper feeds the ball into the air for each girl to attack. Rotate the goalkeeper after 5 minutes. Once every player has been goalkeeper, the game ends with the girl with the most goals as the winner.

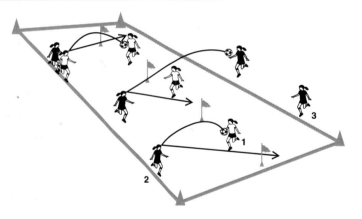

Progressions. Once the girls have confidence heading the ball from 10 yards away, change the game so that the attacker feeds the ball over the goalkeeper's head to her teammate.

Introduce the girls to heading under pressure by moving both players to the same side. The two attackers now compete against each other. The goalkeeper feeds the ball centrally, and each player attempts to score using her head.

Throw, Head, Catch 60

Purpose: To develop confidence competing for and heading the ball against opponents and to improve both offensive and defensive headers	**Equipment:** 4 balls and 4 flags (cones can be used in place of flags)
	Time: 10 to 15 minutes
	Ages: 12 and above
Number of Players: 8 or more	

Use the flags to set up two goals 40 yards apart, and divide the group into two teams. Play four or five girls a side. If you have more than 10 players, break up the group into four teams and have two games going on at the same time. Teams must move the ball up the field using the throw, head, and catch sequence and then score with a header on goal.

One girl throws the ball to a teammate, who heads it for another girl to catch. The same girl cannot head and catch the ball.

If the ball hits the ground or if a team doesn't follow the throw, head, and catch sequence, then possession is turned over to the other team. The team not in possession can attempt to intercept the ball by heading any throws and catching any headers.

Catching a throw isn't allowed by any team and leads to a loss of possession.

CHAPTER 14

Goalkeeping

It's important with beginners and young players that every girl is introduced to goalkeeping in a fun, exciting environment and is made to feel important when given the opportunity to use her hands. The majority of the games here are designed for a whole group or team so that everybody gets the chance to develop and practice the essential techniques of goalkeeping. In the games for 11- and 12-year olds, there are practices and exercises that are designed for developing just one or two players out of your group. These are listed as small-group exercises.

In addition, any shooting or finishing practice outlined earlier that involves the goal can be used to develop and improve the goalkeepers in your group.

Around the World II **61**

Purpose: To develop basic hand-eye-ball coordination, and ball-handling and footwork skills **Number of Players:** Any	**Equipment:** 1 ball per girl **Time:** 5 to 10 minutes **Ages:** 4 to 6

Create an area 20 yards by 20 yards as your world. Have the girls move around the area, side-stepping and bouncing the soccer ball with two hands. Each side of the area is named after a country: England, United States, Japan, and Australia. When that country name is called out, the girls must move to that particular side as quickly as possible. They can only move around the area by side stepping and bouncing the ball with two hands every second step.

While the girls are moving around between countries, call out "High" or "Low." If you call out "High," they must throw the ball straight up in the air and catch it at its highest point. If you call out "Low," they must roll the ball away and then scoop it back up.

When the girls arrive at each country, they amaze everybody by showing how good they are with their handling skills. They must perform each skill five times. At England they move the ball around their back; at the United States they move the ball in and out of their legs in a figure eight; at Japan they throw the ball straight up in the air and catch it; and at Australia they place the ball on the ground and collapse on top of it.

Handling Races 62

Purpose: To develop basic hand-eye ball coordination and ball-handling skills	**Equipment:** 1 ball per group
	Time: 10 to 15 minutes
	Ages: 4 to 6
Number of Players: Any number in groups of 2	

In groups of two players, girls race to be the first to complete a variety of ball-handling challenges. Award points to the first three teams.

Races 1 and 2: Both girls stand back to back and move the ball around their bodies from right to left using just their hands. They must do this 15 times without dropping the ball. If the ball is dropped, they must start again. In the second race they move the ball from left to right.

Races 3 and 4: The girls stand back to back and move the ball through their legs and then over their heads. One girl always moves the ball from her legs to above her head, and the other always moves the ball from above her head to her legs. They must do this 15 times without the ball hitting the ground. If the ball hits the ground, they must start again. In the fourth race the roles are reversed.

Races 5 and 6: The girls stand 5 yards apart facing each other. One girl rolls the ball along the ground. Her partner scoops up the ball, brings it into her body, and throws it back for her teammate to catch in the air. They must repeat the sequence 15 times without dropping the ball. If they drop the ball, they must start again. In the sixth race the roles are reversed.

Home Alone 63

Purpose: To practice catching the ball and stopping shots using a variety of techniques	outside and 8 flags (cones can be used in place of flags)
	Time: 15 to 20 minutes
Number of Players: 8 or more	**Ages:** 7 to 8
Equipment: 1 ball for each girl on the	

This fun goalkeeper game is based on the popular movie. Use the flags to create an area 20 yards by 20 yards. In the middle set up a smaller square 5 yards by 5 yards as the house. Select four girls who will each protect a side of the smaller square, and spread the remaining girls around the outside of the large area. The four girls are home alone and must protect the house from thieves by using their goalkeeping skills. The girls on the outside are the thieves and have 4 minutes to break into the house by shooting soccer balls through the square. Change the goalkeepers every 4 minutes.

Progression. Change the size of both areas to modify the difficulty and the power of the shots that need saving. Practice distribution by having the thieves throw the balls through the square instead of shooting them.

One-on-One Diving 64

Purpose: To introduce and develop diving saves	Equipment: 1 ball and 4 cones per group
Number of Players: Any number in groups of 2	Time: 10 to 15 minutes
	Ages: 7 to 8

This is a great way to introducing the technique of diving. Use the cones to create two small goals 10 yards apart. Each goal should be 5 yards wide. Each girl begins on her knees and tries to roll the ball past her opponent and score a goal. From a kneeling position the defending goalkeeper must dive to her side to make the save. Play for 4 minutes and then switch partners.

Progression. Increase the distance between the two goals, and have the girls play the game from a crouching position.

Keeper Rapid Fire 65

Purpose: To improve diving saves and stopping shots and to develop keeper distribution	Equipment: 4 balls, 4 cones, and 5 flags (cones can be used in place of flags)
Number of Players: 12	Time: 15 to 20 minutes
	Ages: 9 to 10

Use the flags to set up four goals alongside each other. Play the Numbers Game (see Game 5 on page 135) to get the girls into groups of three players, with each girl numbering herself 1, 2, or 3. Player 1 goes into the goal as the goalkeeper while players 2 and 3 stand on either side of the goal at cones placed 15 yards away. They have a 4-minute rapid-fire round to see how many balls they can throw, roll, or shoot past the goalkeeper into the goal. They get three points if they score from a throw or a roll and one point if they score from a shot. If the goalkeeper makes a save, she turns and rolls the ball to the other attacker. After an attacker scores or misses, her partner must first retrieve the ball before taking her turn. Rotate the goalkeeper every 4 minutes. Once every player has been in the goal, the girl with the most points is the winner.

Keeper Wars—Small Group 66

Purpose: To practice footwork, stop shots, and improve goalkeeper distribution	**Equipment:** 4 balls and 4 flags (cones can be used in place of flags)
Number of Players: 2	**Time:** 5 to 10 minutes
	Ages: 10 to 12

Create an area 20 yards long by 15 yards wide, and at each end use the flags to set up an age-appropriate goal. Each girl defends a goal and takes a turn at trying to score on her opponent by shooting, throwing, or punting the ball. When a save is made or a goal is scored, the defending keeper must immediately collect the ball and attack her opponent's goal. The girls are not allowed to take more than three steps with the ball and can't hold onto it for longer than 6 seconds. After 5 minutes of play, the girl with the most goals is the winner.

Progression. Introduce a third player as an attacker who follows up every shot, throw, or punt for both goalkeepers. This places greater emphasis on holding onto the ball and also develops the game-like reactions of making the second save.

Drive Back 67

Purpose: To improve punting accuracy and power	**Equipment:** 1 ball per group
Number of Players: Any number in groups of 2	**Time:** 10 to15 minutes
	Ages: 11 and older

This is a great game for developing the technique, accuracy, and power needed for goalkeepers to punt the ball. Divide the group into pairs and position them 10 yards either side of the halfway line. The girls therefore begin 20 yards apart. The game begins with the first girl punting the ball toward her partner. The receiving keeper attempts to catch the ball before it bounces. If she catches it before the bounce, she moves forward 10 steps before punting the ball back in the opposite direction. If she's unable to catch it, she must punt the ball from wherever it landed. If the punt goes off at an angle and crosses into the area where another group is playing, the receiving girl can advance as far forward as the point from which that punt was taken. Each girl attempts to drive her partner back over the goal line.

Numbered Saves—Small Group 68

Purpose: To improve footwork, reactions, and ability to stop shots	**Equipment:** 10 balls and 1 goal
	Time: 10 to 15 minutes
Number of Players: 2 to 4	**Ages:** 12 and older

This is a great practice and is best used for training two, three, or four goalkeepers. This explanation describes a game with three keepers. Give each girl the number 1, 2, or 3 and position the girls in front of the goal so that player 1 is in front of player 2, and player 2 is in front of player 3.

The coach stands 12–18 yards away with plenty of soccer balls and makes a variety of strikes on the goal. Adjust this distance depending on the ability of the players. If you have an assistant coach or a forward available, he or she can make the strike on goal, so that you can observe and coach the goalkeepers more closely. Just before each strike, call out a number to announce which goalkeeper will make the save. The two other girls must quickly move out the way so that the goalkeeper can position herself to make the save. If the ball hits either of the other girls, the goalkeeper must react and save any rebounds. Change the order of the girls every 3 minutes.

10 Wins—Small Group 69

Purpose: To develop and maintain goalkeeper concentration and confidence	**Equipment:** 10 balls and 1 goal
	Time: 10 to 15 minutes
	Ages: 12 and older
Number of Players: 2	

Goalkeepers can win or lose the game for the team. They're the last line of defense, so any mistakes on their part will likely lead to a goal. With this is in mind, goalkeepers need to be able to learn quickly from any mistakes or goals conceded and move on, maintaining the focus and confidence needed to make the next save. You don't want them thinking or worrying about the last goal or mistake. For the majority of young female goalkeepers, this ability to maintain focus and confidence must be developed. This is a very simple game to help girls learn and develop some of these mental requirements.

One girl or coach is the striker and is positioned on the edge of the penalty area with plenty of soccer balls. Using a variety of techniques, the striker attempts to shoot and score. If the striker scores she gets one goal, but if the goalkeeper makes a save she gets one goal. If the shot is off target, nobody gets any points. The first player to reach 10 goals is the winner. It's important that the striker shoots quickly one ball after the other, so that when a goal is conceded the goalkeeper is forced to immediately forget about it and focus in on making the next save. Halfway through, stop the game to point out and correct any technical errors.

Possession and Defending

Possession

As soon as your team has reached a level where the girls can control and pass the ball, defenders can be introduced into games so that basic possession can be developed. Being able to possess the ball is one of the key components in developing a successful team. If you have the ball, the opposition can't score against you. Initially possession should be introduced in the form of simple games of keep-away, where a group of girls keep the ball away from one or more defenders. To avoid just keeping the ball for the sake of it, they should then be introduced to possessing the ball for a purpose, such as possession leading to an attack.

All the games and exercises listed here can be used for any group of girls, but the size of the playing area, the number of touches, and the number of defenders should be changed depending on ability.

Dog Pound II 70

Purpose: To improve dribbling skills and develop short passing and possession	**Equipment:** 1 ball per girl
	Time: 5 to 10 minutes
	Ages: 7 to 8
Number of Players: 8 or more	

Create an area 30 yards long by 20 yards wide as the dog pound. The girls work in groups of two players, passing and moving around inside the area. Select two girls to be the dogcatchers, who attempt to steal the soccer balls and kick them out of the dog pound as quickly as possible. When a ball has been kicked out, the two girls who were playing with it immediately provide support and passing options to any of the other groups. When all the balls

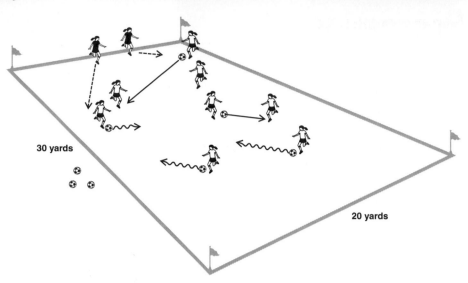

30 yards

20 yards

have been kicked out, the clock stops. Give every pair a chance at being the dogcatchers and see who can set the fastest time.

Four-on-One World Cup 71

Purpose: To develop small-group possession in a restricted area	**Equipment:** 2 balls and 8 cones
	Time: 10 to 15 minutes
Number of Players: 10	**Ages:** 7 to 9

Use the cones to create two squares 12 yards by 12 yards in size. Divide the group into two teams of five girls and place each team in a square. The teams represent two Women's World Cup soccer teams, USA and China. One girl from each team puts on a bib and goes into the other team's area. Each team has to keep the ball away from the defender for 3 minutes. Every time the ball leaves the area due to a poor pass or loss of control, the defender gets a goal for her country. She also gets a goal every time she gains possession of the ball. After 3 minutes the defenders return to their home country, and two other girls become defenders. Each girl defends for 3 minutes. When everybody has defended, the team with the most goals is the Women's World Cup winner.

Three-on-One World Cup

See Game 38 on page 153. This game can be used to improve player movement without the ball, first touch, and passing, while developing small-group possession.

Four-on-Two Intercept 72

Purpose: To develop player movement, first touch, and passing and to improve group possession
Number of Players: 12, in groups of 6

Equipment: 1 ball and 4 flags per group (cones can be used in place of flags)
Time: 10 to 15 minutes
Ages: 9 to 12

Use the flags to create two squares 20 yards by 20 yards in size. Split the group into two teams of six players. Two girls from each team put on bibs and go into the other team's area to defend for 4 minutes. The four other girls position themselves around the outside of the square. They have to pass the ball through the area from one side of the square to another, while the two defenders try to intercept the passes. The defenders are not allowed outside the area. If the ball stops, if a player on the outside makes more than three touches, or if the defenders get possession of the ball, then one point is given to the defending team. After 4 minutes the defenders return to their group and switch with two other girls. When everybody has spent 4 minutes defending, the team with the most points is the winner.

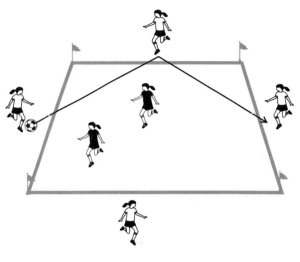

Progressions. Change the size and shape of the area to encourage longer passes.

Reduce the number of touches each girl is allowed.

Four-on-Two Competition

See Game 23 on page 147. This game can be used to improve small-group possession in a restricted area.

Four-Goal Soccer 73

Purpose: To maintain possession of the ball while learning to switch the ball from one side of the field to another
Number of Players: 12

Equipment: 1 ball and 8 flags (cones can be used in place of flags)
Time: 15 to 20 minutes
Ages: 11 and up

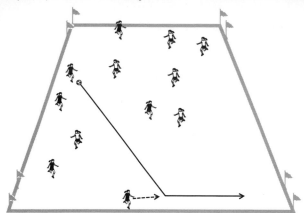

Use the flags to create an area 40 yards by 40 yards and set up two small goals at each end. Divide the girls into teams of six players, and give each team two goals to defend and two goals to attack. There are no goalkeepers. Encourage the girls to keep possession of the ball and attack the goal where there's the most space. If the defenders move to defend one goal, players should quickly switch the ball and attack the goal on the other side of the area.

Sectional Possession 74

Purpose: To maintain possession of the ball in a controlled area while moving the ball up the field; also, to encourage movement off the ball and to develop team fitness	**Number of Players:** 12 **Equipment:** 1 ball, 6 cones, and 4 flags (cones can be used in place of flags) **Time:** 20 minutes **Ages:** 12 and up

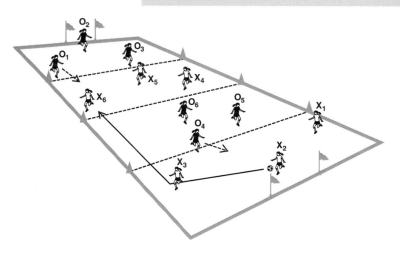

Use the cones to set up four sections running across the soccer field, and use the flags to indicate a goal at each end. Divide the girls into teams of six players, and position three girls in every section. Each team has a defensive section and an attacking section. The defenders must pass the ball over or through their opponent's section to their attacking teammates, who then try to score. Initially one girl is allowed to move and defend against the team in possession, so that a three-on-one situation is created in each section.

For example, when the ball is in X's defensive section, O_4 can go in and try to win the ball back. If O_4 gets the ball, she can score. X's must keep possession and pass the ball across to their attacking section. Once the ball is in X's attacking section, O_1 can go in and try to win the ball back. If O_1 gets the ball, she can pass it straight to her attackers.

This drill may take a few minutes to develop. For the first two to three minutes confusion may reign among defenders, but once they get the hang of it the ball moves quickly from each section, eventually involving all players. The defenders must stay in their own sections, blocking passing lanes and intercepting passes.

Progression Increase the number of girls who can move from one section to another. When the ball is in the defensive section, allow an attacking player from the same team to move into the opponent's section to receive the ball. X_4 can find the space between the opposition and move in to receive the ball.

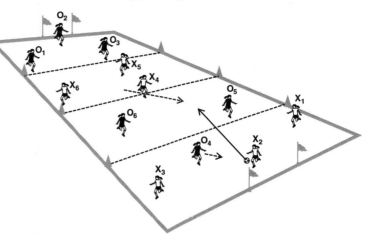

Five-Pass Scoring 75

Purpose: To maintain possession of the ball through short- and long-range passes in an unrestricted area **Number of Players:** 8 or more	**Equipment:** 1 ball **Time:** 10 to 15 minutes **Ages:** 12 and up

Divide the group into two teams who play against each other on half the field. If you have an odd number of players, select one girl to be the floater. She plays on the team in possession. Every time one team makes five consecutive passes, they score a goal. Discuss when to play a quick short pass, when to play longer passes, and when to switch the play. The winner is the first team to score 10 goals.

Progression Increase the pressure on the team in possession by reducing the size of the area and the number of touches each girl is allowed.

End-Zone Soccer 76

Purpose: To keep possession of the ball while trying to attack a specific area of the field **Number of Players:** 12	**Equipment:** 1 ball and 8 flags (cones can be used in place of flags) **Time:** 20 to 25 minutes **Ages:** 12 and up

Use the flags to create an area 50 yards long by 30 yards wide, and at each end set up a small 5-yard end zone. Divide the girls into teams of five players, and select two girls to be floaters. The two floaters play on whichever team has possession. The teams score a goal by passing the ball to a player in an end zone. Once they've scored in one end zone, they try to keep possession and score by passing the ball to another teammate in the other end

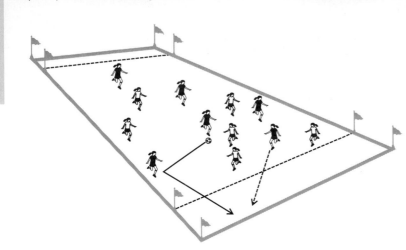

zone. The girls aren't allowed to dribble into the end zone. Initially only players from the team in possession can move into the end zone.

Progressions. Remove the two floaters so that the teams are now even and play six-on-six.

Allow the defending team to also enter the end zone so that there's increased pressure on the team in possession.

Defending

Goldilocks and the Bear 77

Purpose: To introduce individual defensive stance and positioning	**Equipment:** 1 ball per group and 4 cones
Number of Players: Any number in groups of 2	**Time:** 5 to 10 minutes
	Ages: 6 to 7

This is a fun adventure game to introduce defending and the defensive stance to beginners. Use the cones to create an area 20 yards by 20 yards as the forest. Divide the team into groups of two players. One girl has the ball at her feet and is the bear; the other girl is Goldilocks. The bear has 3 minutes to dribble around with the ball and catch Goldilocks as many times as possible by tagging her on the shoulder. After 3 minutes the roles are reversed. Goldilocks must avoid the bear by moving sideways and shuffling backward around the area. Explain to the girls that at no time should they ever turn their back on a bear. Have the girls switch partners and repeat the game. Emphasis is on developing the correct defensive stance to avoid being caught, and watching the ball, not the attacker.

Progression. Goldilocks now has possession of the ball and must dribble as far away from the bear as possible. The bear must follow as closely as possible. When the coach shouts "Freeze" both girls must stop exactly where they are. If the bear (defender) is close enough to touch Goldilocks (the attacker) on the shoulder, the defender gets one point. If she's too far away, the attacker is awarded one point. Play for 3 minutes and then switch roles. The emphasis now is on the defender tracking and staying as close as possible to the attacker.

Home Alone II 78

Purpose: To develop individual defensive positioning with emphasis on how to win or clear the ball
Number of Players: 8 or more

Equipment: 6 balls, 4 cones, and 4 flags (cones can be used in place of flags)
Time: 10 to 15 minutes
Ages: 6 to 7

This fun defending game is based on the popular movie. Use the flags to create an area 20 yards by 20 yards, and in the middle use the cones to set up a smaller square 5 yards by 5 yards as the house. Select four girls who will each protect one side of the smaller square, and spread the remaining girls around the outside of the large area. The four girls are home alone and must

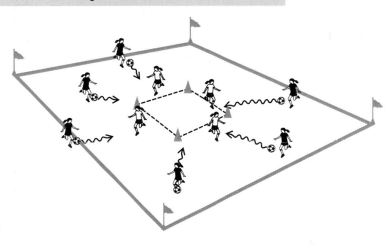

defend the house from the thieves by kicking the balls away. The remaining girls on the outside are the thieves and have 4 minutes to break into the house by dribbling from the outside area into the smaller square and performing a drag back (see page 49) or stop turn (see page 52). Change the defenders every 4 minutes. The defenders with the lowest score against them are the winners.

One-on-One to a Ball 79

Purpose: To improve individual defending with emphasis on when and how to win back possession of the ball
Number of Players: Any number in groups of 2

Equipment: 1 ball per girl
Time: 3 to 5 minutes
Ages: 7 to 10

Create an area 30 yards by 30 yards and divide the team into groups of two players. Both girls in each pair have a ball and begin standing together. One girl kicks her ball about 10–15 yards away and becomes the defender. As soon as the ball has stopped rolling, the second girl becomes an attacker and attempts to dribble her soccer ball and score by hitting the first target ball. If the defending girl gets possession of her partner's ball, she then becomes the attacker. The game is continuous until the target ball is hit, and the girl who hit it gets a point. Then the second girl kicks her ball into space to restart the game. The defender must be encouraged to apply high pressure and win back possession of the ball as far away from the target ball as possible. If she just drops back and stands in front of the ball, automatically award a point to the attacker.

Kick Out

See Game 4 on pages 134–35.

One-on-One to Small Goals 80

Purpose: To improve individual defending, with emphasis on how to defend the goal and how to win back possession of the ball	**Equipment:** 1 ball and 4 cones per group
	Time: 3 to 5 minutes
Number of Players: Any number in groups of 2	**Ages:** 8 to 9

Use the cones to create two small goals 20 yards apart. The goals should be 3 yards wide. One girl in each pair passes the ball to her opponent 20 yards away and becomes a defender (1). The receiving girl becomes the attacker and tries to score in the other girl's goal (2, 3). The defender attempts to steal the ball and score in the opposite goal. After every point is scored, roles are reversed. Place emphasis on closing down the attacker quickly, the defensive stance, being patient, and recognizing when to steal the ball.

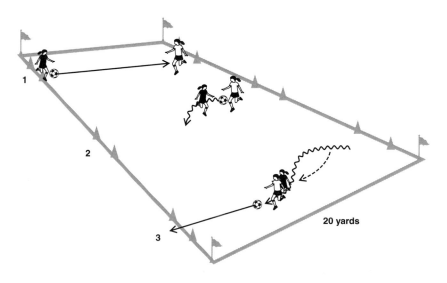

One-on-One to a Line

See Game 12 on page 140. This game can be used to improve individual defending and to increase the role of the first defender.

Two-on-Two to a Line 81

Purpose: To teach defending in pairs and introduce the role of the supporting second defender **Number of Players:** 8 or more in groups of 2	**Equipment:** 2 balls and 6 flags (cones can be used in place of flags) **Time:** 10 to 15 minutes **Ages:** 10 and above

This is a great exercise for teaching the roles of the first and second defender. Use the flags to create two adjoining squares 20 yards by 20 yards. Divide the group into teams of two players. Two teams start on opposite end lines in the same square (1). The defending team begins by passing the ball on the ground across the area. They can defend as soon as an attacking player touches the ball. The attacking team must dribble or use combination play (2) to get past the defenders and score by dribbling across the end line. If the defenders win possession of the ball, they attempt to score by dribbling across the opposite end line. Whenever a goal is scored or the ball goes out of the area, the teams switch roles.

Two-on-Two to Small Goals 82

Purpose: To improve pressuring and covering with the first and second defenders, with emphasis on positioning to cover forward-passing lanes	**Number of Players:** 8 or more in groups of 2 **Equipment:** 2 balls and 16 cones **Time:** 10 to 15 minutes **Ages:** 11 and above

This is a more advanced game for teaching defensive positioning. Use the cones to create two adjoining squares 20 yards by 20 yards and set up a small goal in each corner. The goals should be 2 yards wide. Divide the group into teams of two players. Each team is responsible for defending two goals. The

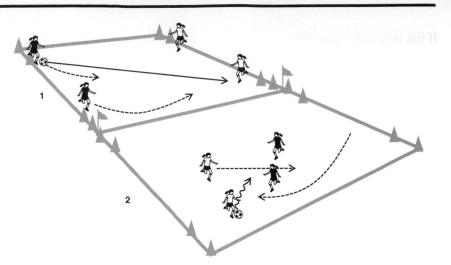

defending team begins by passing the ball on the ground across the area (1). They can defend as soon as an attacking player touches the ball. The attacking team must dribble or use combination play (2) to create space and score on either goal. If the defenders win possession of the ball, they attempt to score in either of the opposite goals. Defenders should close down the attacker with the ball, be aware of pressure and cover, and also curve runs and position themselves to cover direct passing lanes to the goal.

Three-on-Three to a Line 83

Purpose: To improve the roles of the first and second defenders and introduce the balancing third defender **Number of Players:** 6	**Equipment:** 1 ball and 4 cones **Time:** 10 to 15 minutes **Ages:** 12 and above

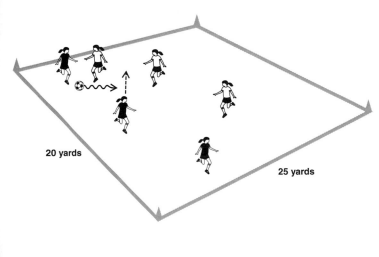

20 yards

25 yards

This is a great exercise for teaching the role of the third defender and the importance of maintaining balance when defending. Use the cones to create an area 25 yards wide by 20 yards long. Divide the group into teams of three players. Both teams start on opposite end lines. The defending team begins by passing the ball on the ground across the area. They can defend as soon as any attacking player touches the ball. The attacking team tries to score by dribbling across the defenders' end line.

If the defenders win possession of the ball, they attempt to score by dribbling across the opposite end line. Whenever a goal is scored or the ball goes out of play, the teams switch defensive roles.

Defending Gates 84

Purpose: To develop team defensive shape	**Equipment:** 1 ball, 6 cones, and 4 flags
	Time: 20 to 25 minutes
Number of Players: 12	**Ages:** 12 and above

This is a controlled game used to teach defensive shape to the whole team. Create a soccer field 40 yards wide by 50 yards long. Use the flags to indicate one goal at each end. Play five-on-five or six-on-six with a goalkeeper on each team. On the halfway line, use the cones to set up three small gates 5 yards wide. Before each team can attack to the goal, they must dribble the ball through any of the small gates. If possession of the ball is won back in the defending team's half, the attacking team can advance attack straight to the goal, without needing to come back through a gate. Emphasize that the defending team should stay compact, deny penetration at the gates, and shift as a unit when the ball is switched. Coaches should look at and highlight to the players the defensive shape when the attack is through an outer gate versus the central gate and the positioning of the balancing defenders.

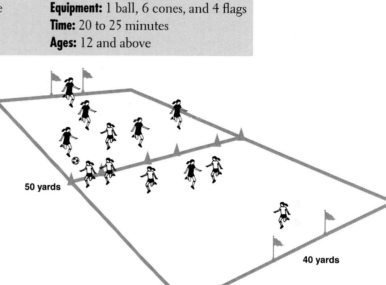

50 yards

40 yards

Progression. Allow the ball to be passed through the gates so defenders learn to track runs and mark players.

APPENDIX: Referee Signals

NFHS Official Soccer Signals

Illustration courtesy National Federation of State High School Associations

Glossary

Attackers: Players who are positioned nearest the opponent's goal and who are responsible for creating and scoring most of the goals; also called forwards or strikers.

Attacking third: The third of the field in front of the goal a team is attacking.

Ball handling: Skills used by a player to move with the ball under control using her feet.

Ball watching: When a player loses sight of an opponent or fails to move to a supporting position, as a result of just watching the movement of the ball.

Chipped pass: A technique used to pass the ball in the air over short and medium distances, over an opponent's head.

Cleats: Soccer-specific footwear with rubber or metal studs to provide better grip.

Combination play: When two or more attacking players combine to move the ball from one area of the field to another.

Corner kick: A kick taken in the corner of the field by the attacking team to restart the game after the defending team has played the ball over its own goal line.

Cross: A pass from the outside of the field to the center or to the opposite side of the field.

Defenders: Players who are positioned nearest to their own goal and who are responsible for preventing the opposition strikers from scoring.

Defending: Techniques and tactics used to prevent the opposition from scoring and to win back possession of the ball.

Defensive stance: The position of the body when defending. The correct stance is like surfing, sideways, on the balls of the feet, with the knees bent and arms out for balance, and the eyes focused on the ball.

Defensive third: The third of the field in front of the goal a team is defending.

Depth: The distance between the most forward and the rearmost outfield player.

Direct free kick: A free kick whereby the attacking team can score by kicking the ball directly into the opponent's goal without another player first touching the ball.

Diving: A technique used by the goalkeeper to save shots that are to her side and are out of her normal range of reach.

Double pass: A combination play where an attacker passes the ball to a teammate who immediately passes it back to her. She then passes it a second time into space for the same teammate to receive.

Dribbling: A technique used by an individual player to move around the field with the ball, using her feet.

Driven pass: A technique used to pass the ball over longer distances using the instep.

Drop ball: A method used by the referee to restart the game when it's been temporarily stopped without the ball going out of play and when neither team has been awarded possession.

Economical training: Training that develops the technical, tactical, physical, and psychological components of soccer at the same time.

End line: The out-of-bounds line at either end of the field, also known as the goal line.

Finishing: Shooting or heading the ball in order to score a goal.

First attacker: The player who has possession of the ball.

First defender: The defender who pressures the attacker with the ball and prevents her from advancing forward. This is normally the player nearest the ball.

Flank: The outside area of the field nearest the sideline.

Footwork: Those skills used by a player to move the ball using her feet.

Formation: A description of the number of players positioned in a team as defenders, midfielders, and attackers.

Forwards: Players on the team who are positioned nearest the opponent's goal and who are responsible for creating and scoring most of the goals; also called attackers or strikers.

Foul: A violation of the rules.

Free kick: An unopposed kick that's awarded when there's a violation of the rules; it is direct or indirect.

Full-sided game: A game using the maximum numbers of players allowed; 11 players on one team compete against 11 players on another team.

Full-sized goal: The maximum size of goal that's allowed (24 feet wide and 8 feet high).

Goal: The target at which each team shoots or heads; a goal is scored when the whole ball crosses the goal line and moves into this area.

Goalkeeper: A special player who guards the goal and who can use her hands to pick up the ball and prevent it from going into the goal. Also known as the goalie.

Goal kick: A kick taken to restart the game when the ball travels over the goal line and out of play and an attacking player was the last to touch it.

Goal line: The out-of-bounds line at either end of the field on which the goals are positioned; also known as the end line.

Goal post: Two vertical posts on either side of the goal between which the ball must travel for a goal to be scored.

Goal side: Position of a defender so that she is closer to the goal she is defending than her marking responsibility.

Halfbacks: Players who are positioned between the attackers and the defenders and who are responsible for moving the ball through the middle of the field; also called midfielders.

Halftime: A short break halfway through the game.

Halfway line: Line running through the middle of the field from either sideline.

Handball: Illegal use of the hand by an outfield player to play the ball.

Handling skills: Those skills performed by a goalkeeper with her hands to catch and block the ball.

Heading: A technique used to play the ball using the head.

High kick: When a ball in the air is kicked with the foot above the waist, at a height that is considered dangerous to surrounding players.

Indirect free kick: A free kick whereby the attacking team cannot score by kicking the ball directly into the opponents' goal; the ball must be touched by at least two different players before a goal can be scored.

In play: When the ball is on the field between both the sidelines and the goal lines; the lines are part of the field of play.

Inside-foot pass: A technique used to pass the ball using the inside of the foot.

Instep: The top of the foot corresponding to the position of the laces of a shoe.

Juggling: A technique used to keep the ball off the ground using different parts of the body and without using the hands.

Keeper gloves: Soccer-specific gloves worn by a goalkeeper to protect her hands and increase her grip on the ball.

Kick-in: In modified games the ball is kicked in when it goes out of bounds, instead of thrown in.

Kicking foot: The foot a player uses to pass, dribble, or shoot the ball.

Kickoff: A kick taken from the center of the field at the start of each half and after a goal is scored, to restart the game.

Lofted pass: A technique in which the instep is used to pass the ball in the air over longer distances.

Marking: Defensive tactics used to defend and guard an opponent.

Midfielders: Players who are positioned between the attackers and the defenders and who are responsible for moving the ball through the middle of the field; also called halfbacks.

Nonkicking foot: The foot a player uses for balancing and aiming when passing or shooting the ball.

Obstruction: A foul in which a player uses her body to illegally block an opponent's path, preventing her from reaching a ball she would otherwise get.

Officials: The referee and assistant referee who enforce the rules of the game.

Offside position: A situation in which an attacking player is in her opponent's half of the field without two defenders being positioned between the attacker and the goal.

One-touch pass: A pass in which a player passes the ball on her first touch without needing to initially get the ball under control.

Out-of-bounds: When the ball leaves the playing area and crosses over the boundary lines.

Outside-foot pass: A technique used to pass the ball using the outside of the foot.

Overarm throw: A technique in which the goalkeeper throws with the arm above shoulder level to quickly distribute the ball to a teammate.

Overhead kick: A spectacular and acrobatic technique where a player jumps and positions her body to kick a ball above her head to a teammate.

Overlap: A combination play where the supporting player makes a run from behind the ball, usually on the outside of the field.

Passing: A technique used to move the ball from one player to another on the same team.

Penalty area: A large area (18 yards long by 44 yards wide), in front of the goal, where the goalkeeper is allowed to use her hands.

Penalty kick: A direct kick taken from inside the penalty area just 12 yards from the goal by an attacking player against the goalkeeper.

Penetrating pass: A forward pass that is played beyond defending players and that moves the attacking team closer to their opponent's goal.

Possession: Keeping the ball away from the opposition.

Punching: A technique used by goalkeepers to knock the ball away in situations when it can't be caught.

Punt: A kick taken by the goalkeeper in which she kicks the ball out of her hands, using her instep.

Recovery runs: Movement of players into defensive positions when possession of the ball is lost.

Scooping: A technique used by the goalkeeper to collect the ball when it's close to or on the ground.

Second attacker: The closest supporting girl to the player who has possession of the ball.

Second defender: The immediate supporting defender who is not directly pressuring the ball, but provides cover and support to the first defender.

Shielding: A technique of using the player's body to protect the ball and maintain possession in limited space when there's no passing option.

Shin guards: Protective pads worn on the shins.

Shooting: A technique used to strike the ball with the foot or head in an attempt to score a goal.

Sideline: The out-of-bounds line on either side of the field that runs from one goal line to the other; also known as the touchline.

6-yard area: A small area (6 yards long by 20 yards wide) in front of the goal, from which all goal kicks are taken; also called the goal area.

Sprain: An injury to a ligament.

Strain: An injury to a muscle or tendon.

Strikers: Players on the team who are positioned nearest the opponent's goal and who are responsible for creating and scoring most of the goals; also called attackers or forwards.

Substitution: Replacing a player on the field with a player who's not currently playing.

Tackling: A technique used to take the ball away from an opponent when defending.

Tactics: The decision making and strategies used in soccer.

Takeover: A combination play where an attacker dribbling with the ball exchanges possession with a teammate moving past her in the opposite direction.

Team manager: A parent who is well organized and manages everything the team does. This can include setting up finances, phone chains, car pools, equipment, and travel plans.

Teammate: A player who's on the same team as someone else.

Team talk: An instructional or motivational talk to a group of players before the game.

Third defenders: The defenders who are farther away from the ball that must provide balance to the defensive situation.

Throw-in: A technique used to put the ball back in play after it's gone out-of-bounds over the sideline.

Time wasting: When one team illegally attempts to take a long time to bring the ball back into play on a restart.

Touchline: The out-of-bounds line on either side of the field that runs from one goal line to the other; also known as the sideline.

Tracking: The movement of a defender when marking an attacker who's making a run without the ball.

Trapping: A catching technique used by the goalkeeper to trap the ball between the body and the arms.

Tryout: A set of exercises and games used to identify players and assess their playing ability.

Volley: A technique used to pass or shoot the ball in the air using just one touch.

Wall pass: A combination play where the attacker with the ball uses a supporting teammate like a wall to play a quick pass around a defender.

Weak foot: The foot a player uses the least and is less competent with.

Width: The distance between the player nearest the left sideline and the player nearest the right sideline.

Winger: An attacking player positioned toward the side of the field who is responsible for creating width in the attack, beating defenders in wide positions, and crossing the ball.

Resources

American Alliance for Health, Physical Education, Recreation and Dance

AAHPERD
1900 Association Dr.
Reston, VA 20191-1598
1-800-213-7193
www.aahperd.org
AAHPERD promotes and supports creative and healthy lifestyles through high-quality programs in health, physical education, recreation, dance, and sport. It provides members with professional development opportunities that increase knowledge, improve skills, and encourage sound professional practices.

American Youth Soccer Organization

AYSO
12501 S. Isis Ave.
Hawthorne, CA 90250
1-800-872-2976
www.soccer.org
AYSO is a nationwide nonprofit organization that develops and delivers quality soccer programs in a fun, family environment. It is a member of the National Association of the United States Soccer Federation and has been the leader in establishing groundbreaking youth soccer programs with over 630,000 youth soccer players and more than 250,000 volunteer coaches, referees, and administrators.

National Association for Girls and Women in Sports

NAGWS
1900 Association Dr.
Reston, VA 20191-1598

1-800-213-7193
www.nagws.org
NAGWS is the leading organization dedicated to addressing issues and promoting opportunities for all girls and women in sport. It develops and delivers equitable and quality sport opportunities for girls and women through relevant research, advocacy, leadership development, educational strategies, and programming in a manner that promotes social justice and change. Since 1899, the National Association for Girls and Women in Sport has championed equal funding, quality, and respect for women's sports programs. These efforts have led to national championship programs in collegiate women's sports and to the passage of Title IX legislation. The NAGWS awards program includes the Pathfinder Awards, honoring those who advocate, recruit, and enhance opportunities for girls and women in sports and sport leadership, and the Presidential Awards, honoring exceptional contributions to the profession and the association.

National Collegiate Athletic Association

NCAA
700 W. Washington St.
P.O. Box 6222
Indianapolis, IN 46206-6222
(317) 917-6222
www.ncaa.org
The NCAA is a voluntary organization through which the nation's colleges and universities govern their athletics programs. It comprises more than 1,250 institutions, conferences, organi-

zations, and individuals committed to the best interests, education, and athletics participation of student-athletes.

National Soccer Coaches Association of America

NSCAA
6700 Squibb Rd., Suite 215
Mission, KS 66202
1-800-458-0678
www.nscaa.com
info@nscaa.com
The NSCAA is the largest coaches' organization in the United States. Since its founding in 1941, it has grown to include more than 17,000 members who coach both males and females at all levels of the sport. In addition to a national rankings program for colleges and high schools, NSCAA offers an extensive recognition program that presents more than 10,000 individual awards every year. It fulfills its mission of coaching education through a nationwide program of clinics and week-long courses, teaching more than 3,000 soccer coaches each year.

Noga Soccer

NOGA Soccer
P.O. Box 262
Garden City, NY 11530
1-800-422-6778
www.nogasoccer.com
NOGA is the leader in soccer and education services. For 30 years the Noga Company has been at the forefront of developing soccer education and programs and continues to provide the ultimate in professional soccer and education services. Noga provides professional coaching, elite player development, club curriculums, educational camps, and world-class international tournaments throughout the Unites States.

Sporting Goods Manufacturers Association

SGMA
200 Castlewood Dr.
North Palm Beach, FL 33408-5696
(561) 842-4100
www.sgma.com
info@sgma.com
SGMA International is the recognized leader in providing the sporting goods industry with statistical reports, trend analysis information, and market segment reports. SGMA's mission is to support their members through programs and strategies that increase sports participation and volunteerism in grassroots sports and to influence public policy.

United States Soccer Federation

USSF
1801 S. Prairie Ave.
Chicago, IL 60616
(312) 808-1300
www.ussoccer.com
The governing body of soccer in all its forms in the United States, USSF has helped chart the course for the sport in the United States for 90 years. In that time, the Federation's mission statement has been simple and clear: to make soccer, in all its forms, a preeminent sport in the United States and to continue the development of soccer at all recreational and competitive levels. USSF was founded in 1913 as one of the world's first organizations to be affiliated with FIFA, the Fédération Inter-

nationale de Football Association, soccer's world governing body.

US Youth Soccer

US Youth Soccer
1717 Firman Dr., Suite 900
Richardson, TX 75081
1-800-4SOCCER
www.usyouthsoccer.org
US Youth Soccer is a nonprofit and educational organization whose mission is to foster the physical, mental, and emotional growth and development of America's youth through the sport of soccer at all levels of age and competition. US Youth Soccer is the largest member of the United States Soccer Federation, the governing body for soccer in the United States with a nationwide body of over 600,000 volunteers and administrators, and over 300,000 dedicated coaches, most of whom also are volunteers. US Youth Soccer registers over 3,000,000 youth players between the ages of 5 and 19. US Youth Soccer is made up of 55 member state associations (one in each state, and two in California, New York, Ohio, Pennsylvania, and Texas). US Youth Soccer

provides a fun, safe, and healthy game for *all kids*—big kids, little kids, tall kids, short kids, young kids, older kids—kids who want to play for one season, kids who want to play for 20 seasons, kids who play strictly for fun, and kids who want to compete at the highest level possible.

Women's United Soccer Association

WUSA
www.wusa.com
WUSA was the world's premier women's professional soccer league. In the 2001 inaugural season, the eight-team league featured the best players from the 1999 U.S. World Cup Championship Team and top-flight international players. Unfortunately, the financial backing did not continue to support the league after the WUSA's third season, and the announcement was made on September 15, 2003, that the league was suspending its operations immediately. A group of former league officers joined with the Player's Association to revive the WUSA in 2004 and beyond.

Index

Numbers in bold refer to pages with photographs or illustrations. The glossary and resources have not been indexed.

About the Author

For the past 12 years Drayson Hounsome has been extensively involved in the development of soccer at every age and level, from beginners to professional players. Since 2001 he has been the head women's soccer coach at the CW Post Campus of Long Island University, and prior to that he was the assistant coach at Molloy College for five years. Hounsome holds a Bachelor of Science degree with honors in Sport Science and Physical Education from England's premier sporting institute, Loughborough University, and has been awarded advanced coaching licenses from the English Football Association (F.A), the United States Soccer Federation (USSF), and the National Soccer Coaches Association of America (NSCAA).